Maryland RV Road Atlas 2025

Detailed Road Maps, Scenic Routes, Curated Itineraries, Campgrounds, and Outdoor Adventures — Your Expert Guide to Coastal Drives, Historical Landmarks, and Hidden Natural Wonders

Colin Westgate

Copyright © 2025 **Colin Westgate**

All Rights Reserved

This book or parts thereof may not be reproduced in any form, stored in any retrieval system, or transmitted in any form by any means—electronic, mechanical, photocopy, recording, or otherwise—without prior written permission of the publisher, except as provided by United States of America copyright law and fair use.

Disclaimer and Terms of Use

The author and publisher of this book and the accompanying materials have used their best efforts in preparing this book. The author and publisher make no representation or warranties with respect to the accuracy, applicability, fitness, or completeness of the contents of this book. The information contained in this book is strictly for informational purposes. Therefore, if you wish to apply the ideas contained in this book, you are taking full responsibility for your actions.

Printed in the United States of America

TABLE OF CONTENT

TABLE OF CONTENT III
INTRODUCTION 1
EMBARK ON YOUR ULTIMATE RV ADVENTURE IN MARYLAND 1
   Why Maryland is a Top Destination for RV Travelers 1
CHAPTER 1 4
PREPARING FOR YOUR MARYLAND RV ROAD TRIP 4
  CHOOSING THE RIGHT RV FOR MARYLAND'S TERRAIN 4
    Choosing the Right RV for Your Maryland Journey 5
  CRAFTING THE PERFECT MARYLAND ROAD TRIP ITINERARY 8
    Scenic Routes, Historic Trails, and Nature-Driven Escapes That Redefine the Open Road 8
  BUDGETING YOUR MARYLAND RV ADVENTURE 12
    Stretching Your Dollars Without Shrinking the Experience 12
CHAPTER 2 16
MARYLAND'S SCENIC ROUTES AND HIGHWAYS 16
  THE CHESAPEAKE COUNTRY SCENIC BYWAY 16
    Dining Delights Along the Byway 19
  THE NATIONAL ROAD (U.S. ROUTE 40) 19
    RV-Friendly Stops Along the National Road 22
    Dining Delights Along the National Road 22
  THE APPALACHIAN MOUNTAINS SCENIC BYWAY 23
    Discovering the Appalachian Mountains Scenic Byway 23
    RV Camping: Embracing the Mountain Wilderness 24
    Dining and Local Flavor 25
CHAPTER 3 26
BEST CAMPGROUNDS AND RV PARKS IN MARYLAND 26
  THE UNFORGETTABLE QUEST FOR THE PERFECT MARYLAND CAMPGROUND 26
    Section 1: The Magic of Maryland's State Parks for RV Campers 26
    Section 2: Top Maryland State Parks for RV Campers 27
    Section 3: Insider Tips for Booking and Enjoying Maryland RV Campgrounds 29
    Section 4: Real Stories from the Road 30
    Section 5: Beyond the Campsites — Exploring Maryland's Surroundings 31
  LUXURY RV RESORTS AND GLAMPING SITES: ELEVATE YOUR MARYLAND CAMPING EXPERIENCE 31
    The Allure of Luxury on the Road 31
    Reflect and Imagine 33
  HIDDEN GEM CAMPGROUNDS AND SECLUDED ESCAPES: FIND YOUR PEACE OFF THE BEATEN PATH .. 34

The Quiet Call of Solitude *34*
Discovering Maryland's Hidden Treasures *34*
Small-Town Charm Meets Quiet Camping *36*

CHAPTER 4 38

MARYLAND'S NATIONAL AND STATE PARKS 38

ASSATEAGUE ISLAND NATIONAL SEASHORE 38
A Personal Journey to Assateague Island *38*
Practical Tips for Your Visit *40*
CATOCTIN MOUNTAIN PARK 42
Discovering the Hidden Gem of Catoctin Mountain *42*
Practical Tips for Visiting Catoctin Mountain Park *45*
CALVERT CLIFFS STATE PARK 45
A Journey Back Through Time at Calvert Cliffs *45*
Camping and RV Options Near Calvert Cliffs *47*
Practical Tips for Visiting Calvert Cliffs *48*

CHAPTER 5 49

OUTDOOR ACTIVITIES AND ADVENTURES IN MARYLAND 49

HIKING AND TRAIL ADVENTURES 49
RV Parks Near Trailheads: Combining Adventure with Comfort *51*
WATER SPORTS AND RIVER ADVENTURES 52
RV Campgrounds with Waterfront Access *55*
Essential Gear and Safety Tips *56*
FISHING AND WILDLIFE WATCHING IN MARYLAND 57
Top Spots for Wildlife Watching *57*
RV Campgrounds for Outdoor Lovers *58*
Essential Wildlife Watching Tips *59*
Essential Fishing Tips for Maryland *59*

CHAPTER 6 60

EXPLORING MARYLAND'S ICONIC CITIES 60

BALTIMORE: CULTURE, HISTORY, AND HARBOR 60
A City That Stole My Breath—And Then Gave It Back *60*
Top RV Parks Near Baltimore: *62*
Quick Travel Tips for Visiting Baltimore in an RV *63*
ANNAPOLIS: MARYLAND'S STATE CAPITAL 64
A City Anchored in History, Drifting in Charm *64*
RV-Friendly Campgrounds Near Annapolis *65*
Annapolis Isn't Just a Place—It's a Feeling *67*
Travel Tips for RVers Exploring Annapolis: *67*
OCEAN CITY: A BEACH LOVER'S PARADISE 68

Where Salt Air Heals, and Memories Live Forever *68*
Best RV Parks Near the Ocean *70*
Tips for RVers Exploring Ocean City *71*

CHAPTER 7 72

HISTORY, CULTURE, AND HERITAGE IN MARYLAND 72

THE CIVIL WAR'S ROLE IN MARYLAND'S HISTORY 72
Where Conflict Carved a State's Soul and Echoes Still Whisper Through the Land .. 72
RV Parks and Civil War Camping Near the Conflict 75
The Battle Beneath the Surface 76

THE LEGACY OF THE CHESAPEAKE BAY 77
Where Water Holds Memory, and Culture Runs as Deep as the Tides 77
RV Campgrounds Near the Bay: Wake Up to Water, Wind, and Wonder 79
Environmental Stewardship: A Bay at a Crossroads 80
The Chesapeake Is a Living Soul 80

NATIVE AMERICAN AND AFRICAN AMERICAN HERITAGE 81
Voices That Shaped the Land, Stories That Refuse to Be Forgotten 81
Other Sites of African American and Native American Heritage in Maryland 83
RV Campgrounds Near Heritage Sites 84
Heritage as a Compass 85

CHAPTER 8 86

MARYLAND'S CULINARY DELIGHTS – CRAB CAKES AND SEAFOOD 86

The Chesapeake Bay: Maryland's Seafood Heartbeat 86
RV-Friendly Seafood Stops: Dining on the Go 87
FARM-TO-TABLE DINING 88
BREWERIES AND DISTILLERIES 90

CHAPTER 9 93

RV SAFETY AND MAINTENANCE IN MARYLAND 93

NAVIGATING MARYLAND'S ROADS SAFELY 93
Strategies for urban RV driving: 94
RV Road Safety Advice for Tourists Driving During Peak Seasons 95
Tips for varying road conditions: 96
Tips for Safe RV Driving in Maryland 96
MAINTAINING YOUR RV WHILE ON THE ROAD IN MARYLAND 97
RV Service Centers Across Maryland 98
WEATHER AND SEASONAL CONSIDERATIONS FOR RV TRAVEL IN MARYLAND 100
RVing in Maryland's Summer Heat 101
Surviving Maryland's Winter in an RV 102

CHAPTER 10 105

v

HIDDEN GEMS AND OFF-THE-BEATEN-PATH ADVENTURES 105

Exploring Maryland's Small Towns and Villages 105
- The Allure of the Road Less Traveled 105
- St. Michaels: A Maritime Haven 105
- The Magic of Small Towns 108

Underrated Nature Escapes in Maryland 109
- Seeking Solitude in Nature 109
- Western Maryland Rail Trail: A Journey Through History and Nature 110

Quirky Attractions and Roadside Wonders in Maryland 112
- Embracing the Unconventional 112

CHAPTER 11 115

SEASONAL RV ADVENTURES IN MARYLAND – SUMMER FESTIVALS AND EVENTS 115

When the Open Road Meets Summer Magic 115
- Section 1: Why Maryland in Summer? A Hidden Gem for RV Travelers 115
- Section 2: Top Summer Festivals That Belong on Your RV Bucket List 116
- Section 3: Planning the Ultimate Festival-Focused RV Trip 118
- Section 4: Festival Hacks Only Experienced RVers Know 118
- Section 5: Real Moments on the Road – My Summer of Surprises 119

Autumn Foliage and Harvest Activities in Maryland 119
- The Season That Changed Everything 119
- Catoctin Mountain Park 121
- Scenic Drives Worth the Detour 121
- RV-friendly nearby: Little Bennett Campground 121

Winter Escapes and Cozy Getaways in Maryland 124
- Where the Cold Finds You—and Warms You, Too 124
- Section 1: Why Winter is Maryland's Best-Kept RV Secret 124
- Section 2: Snow-Draped Adventures and Outdoor Wonders 125
- Section 3: RV Parks That Welcome Winter Travelers 125
- Section 4: Cozy Cabins, Fireside Retreats, and Comfort Food 126
- Section 5: Holiday Magic and Festive Small-Town Charm 126
- Section 6: My Coldest, Warmest Night on the Road 127

CHAPTER 12 129

CONCLUSION 129

YOUR UNFORGETTABLE MARYLAND RV JOURNEY 129

Reflecting on Your Maryland Adventure 129
- I. Opening Reflection: My Final Night Under the Maryland Stars 129
- II. The Road That Changed Me: A Recap of Your Maryland RV Odyssey 129
- III. The Seasons of Maryland: Why One Trip Is Never Enough 130
- IV. Why This Journey Mattered (And Still Does) 131
- V. Tips for Returning (Because You Will Want To) 131

VI. Your Next Step: Taking Maryland With You *132*
VII. One Final Thought: This Isn't Goodbye *132*
PLANNING FUTURE RV TRIPS ACROSS MARYLAND 132

INTRODUCTION

EMBARK ON YOUR ULTIMATE RV ADVENTURE IN MARYLAND

What if your next great escape wasn't thousands of miles away—but waiting just beyond your backyard?

What if freedom, discovery, and that long-overdue sense of awe could all be found on a road trip through one of America's most underrated treasures—Maryland?

I remember the first time we packed up the RV with more hope than a plan. My youngest had just finished her last virtual school class of the year, my partner had finally logged off after a marathon of Zoom meetings, and I was burnt out from months of routine that never seemed to change. We were restless. Anxious. Searching for something more than just a vacation—we needed a reset.

We didn't know where we were going, just that we were heading *out*. We rolled toward the Chesapeake Bay with a tank full of gas and hearts full of questions: Would this actually help us reconnect? Could we really unwind with two kids, a dog, and a 30-foot motorhome?

What we found blew us away. We camped under star-filled skies in the Appalachian highlands, traced the echoes of Civil War cannons at Antietam, and watched wild horses roam free on Assateague Island. We wandered cobbled streets in Annapolis, shopped at crab shacks off beaten backroads, and woke up every day to a new view. Somewhere between the winding mountain passes and sunlit boardwalks, we found what we didn't even know we were missing.

That's the magic of Maryland. It's a small state with a giant heart—and whether you're a seasoned RVer or just starting your journey, this place has a way of making you feel both grounded and limitless.

Why Maryland is a Top Destination for RV Travelers

Maryland is a state of contrasts—lush forests and vibrant cities, coastal serenity and historic battlefields, charming small towns and untamed wilderness. In just a few hours' drive, you can cross from the tranquil tides of the Eastern Shore to the rugged heights of the western mountains.

This road atlas is your gateway to exploring it all:

The **Chesapeake Bay**, where sunsets melt over the water and seafood is caught fresh from the dock.

Historic byways that tell the story of America's past through scenic detours.

State parks, hidden waterfalls, and quiet campgrounds tucked away where GPS signals fade and real connection begins.

What to Expect from This RV Road Atlas

Inside, you'll find:

Detailed, RV-friendly **maps of every major route, byway, and scenic drive** across Maryland.

Expert recommendations for campgrounds—from rustic boondocking spots to full-hookup resorts.

Curated **itineraries tailored to every type of traveler**, whether you're chasing adventure, history, or peace and quiet.

Local **insights and hidden gems** you won't find in your average travel brochure.

Making the Most of Your Maryland RV Journey

We'll guide you through:

Choosing the right **RV for your travel style**.

Navigating Maryland's **unique geography and weather**.

Blending urban experiences with wild escapes.

Making unforgettable memories with the people who matter most.

Whether you're planning your first RV road trip or your fiftieth, this atlas isn't just about directions—it's about **rediscovering wonder, forging new traditions, and seeing Maryland through fresh eyes**.

So fire up the engine, roll down the windows, and let's hit the road. Your adventure starts now.

CHAPTER 1

PREPARING FOR YOUR MARYLAND RV ROAD TRIP

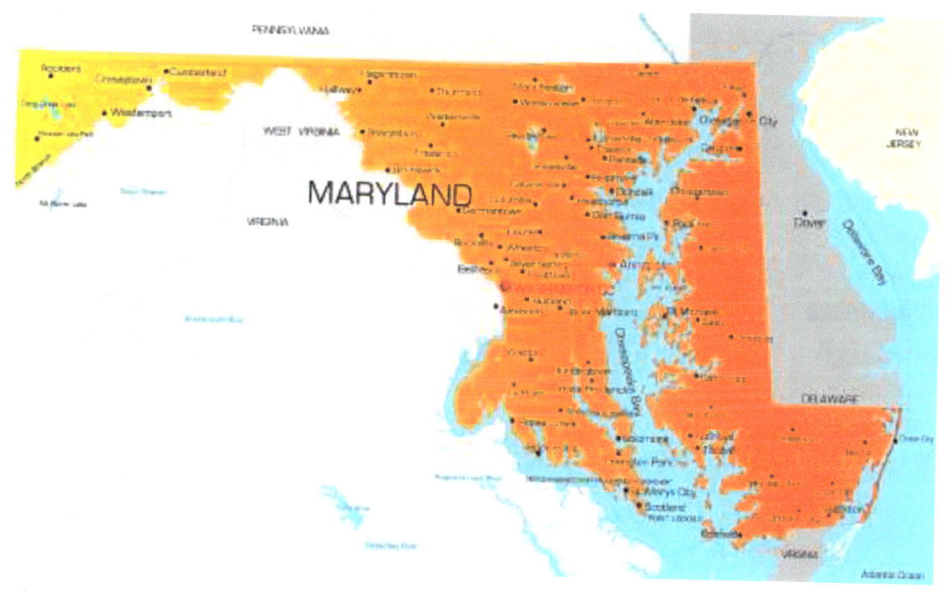

Maryland Map

CHOOSING THE RIGHT RV FOR MARYLAND'S TERRAIN

"Is This Really the Right RV?" – The Question That Almost Derailed Our Trip Before It Even Started

I'll never forget the morning we left. Or, more accurately, the morning we *tried* to leave. The sun had barely risen. Our kids were still rubbing sleep out of their eyes, our dog was already howling in excitement, and I stood outside the driveway with a cold coffee in hand, staring at the gleaming 32-foot Class A motorhome I'd proudly rented a week earlier. It was beautiful. Spacious. Shiny. And within ten minutes of hitting the road... *absolutely terrifying*. The first turn out of our suburban neighborhood felt like trying to do ballet in a bulldozer. I scraped a mailbox. Twice. When we got onto the highway, it swayed in the wind like a sailboat in a storm. By the time we climbed into the hilly stretches of Western Maryland, I was white-knuckled and half-sure we weren't going to make it to the first campground. Have you ever wondered why the trip you dream about becomes the one that tests you the most? Why the adventure you hoped would bring joy instead brings frustration—at least at first? I had chosen the wrong RV. Not because it wasn't high-quality, but because it wasn't *right* for the kind of Maryland road trip we were taking: narrow roads, steep grades, tight turns through historic towns with cobbled streets and low-hanging trees. I was so busy focusing on the dream that I forgot to consider the reality. And that's exactly where this chapter begins. Let's save *you* from that first hard lesson.

Have You Thought About the Type of Maryland Adventure You Want?
Before you choose an RV, ask yourself: Are you planning to spend most of your time exploring **urban landmarks like Baltimore or Annapolis**? Or do you envision winding through **Appalachian switchbacks**, camping in the **Catoctin Mountains**, or parking beachfront on **Assateague Island**? Will you be **staying in one place for a while**, or is this a fast-moving adventure with **new stops every night**? Your answers will determine whether a **motorhome**, **campervan**, or **travel trailer** is your best choice.

Understanding Maryland's Diverse Terrain

Maryland is a small state—but it holds *five distinct geographical regions*, each offering a different driving and camping experience: 1. **The Coastal Plain (Eastern Shore)** – Flat, easy to navigate, but tight rural roads. 2. **The Piedmont Plateau (Central Maryland)** – Rolling hills and suburban congestion. 3. **The Blue Ridge Mountains & Appalachian Region (Western Maryland)** – Steep climbs, winding roads. 4. **Urban Zones (Baltimore, D.C. metro)** – Tight parking, traffic-heavy, limited clearance. 5. **The Chesapeake Bay Area** – Mixed terrain, scenic byways, and frequent ferry crossings. Maryland's variety is what makes it a dream for RVers—*but only if you match your rig to your route.*

Choosing the Right RV for Your Maryland Journey

1. Class A Motorhomes: Spacious But Not Always Suitable

Best for: Long stays in open campgrounds. Flat or gently rolling regions. Travelers who want high luxury and full amenities.

Beware: **Tight mountain roads** and **historic town streets** can be overwhelming. Parking in places like **Annapolis or Frederick** is next to impossible. Fuel efficiency is low.

Personal Tip: "We used a Class A on our first trip and ended up leaving it parked for half the trip, using bikes and Uber. Amazing inside—but useless in small towns or highlands."

2. Class C Motorhomes: The Balanced Choice

Best for: Families or small groups wanting a blend of comfort and maneuverability. State parks and moderate elevation drives.

Pros: More compact, fits in most state park RV spots. Easier to handle than Class A.

Cons: Still bulky for **tight historic areas** like St. Michaels or Ellicott City. Reflection Question: *Have you thought about what it will feel like to drive your RV—not just sleep in it?*

3. Campervans (Class B): For the Adventurous & Nimble

Best for: Couples or solo travelers seeking spontaneity. Those who want to *go off-grid* and don't need full hookups.

Pros: **Perfect for small roads and backcountry adventures**. Can easily park in cities, trailheads, even parallel park downtown.

Cons: Limited storage and amenities. Not ideal for families.

Power Tip: "Our second trip? A campervan. It changed everything. We drove down backroads we didn't even know existed and camped in hidden parks we'd never have reached in a big rig."

4. Travel Trailers: Flexible But Requires Confidence

Best for: Travelers with experience towing. Those who want to park and explore with a separate vehicle.

Pros: More space per dollar than motorhomes. Detachable for day trips with a tow vehicle.

Cons: Steep learning curve for towing and reversing. **Can be difficult on mountainous or narrow terrain.**

Quick Advice: *New to towing? Try practicing in a big empty parking lot before hitting real roads.*

Matching RV Size to Maryland's Campgrounds

Many of Maryland's **state parks** and **county campgrounds** have **size limits** (often 30 feet or less). Don't assume your dream rig will fit anywhere—always check **length limits** when booking sites.

"We booked a week at Patapsco Valley State Park, only to arrive and find out our rig couldn't fit through the gate. That was a $400 mistake."

Understanding Local Driving Conditions

I-68 through Western Maryland has steep grades and requires lower gears—*especially in winter*.

Bay Bridge (US-50) can be intimidating for high-profile vehicles in windy weather.

Route 213 is stunningly scenic but filled with low-clearance bridges and sharp turns.

Downtown Annapolis and Baltimore = historic charm + modern RV headaches. Don't just plan your *destinations*—plan your *routes*.

Weather: The Hidden Factor in RV Travel

Maryland weather can shift dramatically: Summer brings **heat and humidity** on the Eastern Shore. Fall can mean **foggy, slick roads** in the mountains. Winter snow in Western Maryland surprises many. Spring rains can flood roads near the Chesapeake. Always **check weather and road conditions**—especially in early spring and late fall.

Plan Like a Pro, Travel Like a Local

Choosing the right RV isn't just about what looks best online—it's about *knowing* what kind of journey you're about to take and preparing accordingly. Maryland is dynamic. It's not the kind of place where one-size-fits-all. But that's what makes it so rewarding.

So... **What kind of traveler do you want to be? What kind of memories are you hoping to make?** Let's make sure the RV you choose helps you get there—not hold you back.

CRAFTING THE PERFECT MARYLAND ROAD TRIP ITINERARY

Scenic Routes, Historic Trails, and Nature-Driven Escapes That Redefine the Open Road

Have you ever sat behind the wheel of your RV, ready to go, engine rumbling, snacks packed... but you have no idea where to actually begin? That was us. Sitting in a gas station parking lot somewhere on the edge of Route 50, maps spread across the dash, bickering over whether to head toward the bay or the mountains. We had the time, the rig, the weather—but no direction. It's funny how freedom can feel paralyzing without a plan. And let's be honest: nothing kills the vibe faster than indecision on Day One. That's why this chapter exists—to make sure you never feel that lost. Here, you'll find carefully curated itineraries built around what makes Maryland shine: its unmatched diversity. You'll discover not just where to go, but *why* to go there—and how to shape your trip around what *you* love most. Whether you're drawn to tranquil waters, mountain hikes, or stories carved into cobblestone streets, Maryland has a route that feels like it was made just for you.

Maryland's Must-Drive Scenic Routes

Let's start with the good stuff: roads that will take your breath away. Not all routes are created equal, and Maryland's scenic byways are more than just pretty drives—they're immersive experiences. If you're looking for postcard-worthy landscapes, charming small towns, and unforgettable pit stops, consider these road-tested favorites:

Chesapeake Country Scenic Byway (US-50/MD-213/MD-18): This is Maryland's crown jewel for coastal drives. It hugs the Eastern Shore, passing through charming waterfront towns like Chestertown and Cambridge, and lets you soak in the serenity of the Chesapeake Bay. Must-stop: the ferry ride at Oxford-Bellevue and crabbing shacks in Rock Hall.

Historic National Road (US-40): America's first federally funded highway begins in Baltimore and winds its way through Ellicott City, Frederick, and Cumberland. This is a dream route for history buffs, antique lovers, and anyone who appreciates 18th-century architecture paired with small-town charm.

Historic National Road (US-40)

Catoctin Mountain Scenic Byway (US-15): A nature lover's favorite, this route runs past Catoctin Mountain Park and offers access to stunning hikes and mountain views. Bonus: it's home to Camp David (no, you can't visit—but it's cool to drive past).

Journey Through Hallowed Ground Byway (MD-194 to US-15): If you want a soul-stirring experience, this drive weaves you through Civil War history, past battlefields, memorials, and towns that feel paused in time.

Mountain Maryland Scenic Byway (I-68/US-40 Alt): Ready for a jaw-dropping climb into the Appalachians? This route takes you west, through Deep Creek Lake, Savage River State Forest, and the quaint town of Frostburg. It's pure rustic adventure, perfect for those who want pine-scented air and silence.

Itinerary #1: Chesapeake Bay Charm – A 5-Day Waterfront Escape

This route is for the traveler who craves coastal breeze, crab feasts, and bayside serenity.

Day 1: Start in Annapolis. Explore the Naval Academy, stroll the historic district, and enjoy dinner at a dockside oyster bar. Overnight at a nearby RV park with bay access.

Day 2: Drive across the Bay Bridge to Kent Island. Stop at Terrapin Nature Park, then head to Chestertown for antique shops and colonial charm.

Day 3: Meander down to Cambridge and visit the Harriet Tubman Underground Railroad Visitor Center. Camp near Blackwater National Wildlife Refuge—sunset here is unforgettable.

Day 4: Continue south to Solomons Island. Kayak the Patuxent River, eat freshly caught rockfish, and park your RV at a waterfront site.

Day 5: Head inland to St. Mary's City for a dose of early colonial history before looping back toward Annapolis.

Itinerary #2: Footsteps Through Time – Maryland's Historic Heart in 6 Days
Perfect for families, educators, or anyone fascinated by America's past.

Day 1: Begin in Baltimore with Fort McHenry, birthplace of the national anthem. Then visit the B&O Railroad Museum.

Day 2: Head west to Ellicott City. Tour the historic downtown and check out the 19th-century flour mill.

Day 3: Drive to Frederick. Walk Civil War trails and visit Monocacy National Battlefield.

Day 4: Explore Antietam National Battlefield. Stay overnight near Hagerstown.

Day 5: Head to Harpers Ferry (just across the West Virginia border), then return to Maryland via Brunswick for scenic river views.

Day 6: Wrap up in Annapolis with a guided historical walking tour and a boat ride across the bay.

Itinerary #3: Appalachian Escape – 7 Days of Nature, Solitude, and Mountain Air
This one's for the hiker, the forest bather, the campfire soul.

Day 1: Begin in Cumberland and stock up on supplies. Hike along the Great Allegheny Passage.

Day 2: Head to Deep Creek Lake. Paddle in the morning, bike in the afternoon.

Day 3: Drive to Swallow Falls State Park. Camp beneath hemlocks and fall asleep to rushing water.

Day 4: Explore Backbone Mountain and take in the state's highest point.

Day 5: Visit Frostburg and enjoy a scenic train ride.

Day 6: Camp off-grid in Savage River State Forest. Nothing but trees and stars.

Day 7: Loop back to Cumberland, stopping at Rocky Gap State Park for one last hike.

Themed Road Trips: Tailoring the Experience to You

Sometimes the best trips aren't defined by geography, but by passion. Consider designing your trip around a personal theme:

The Outdoor Explorer: Combine Assateague Island, Catoctin Mountain, and the Appalachian Trail access points. Prioritize kayaking, hiking, and wildlife viewing.

The History Hunter: Follow colonial and Civil War-era paths from Annapolis to Antietam, ending at Mount Vernon (just outside the border).

The Culture Connoisseur: Focus on Baltimore's museums, Frederick's art galleries, and the food and music scene in Takoma Park.

The Waterway Wanderer: Build your route around Maryland's rivers—Potomac, Patuxent, Severn—and sleep within earshot of the waves each night.

Creating Your Own Maryland Itinerary

Not seeing your perfect route yet? No problem. Maryland's scale makes it ideal for DIY routes: you can create a custom 3-day loop or a 2-week full-state journey with ease. Start with your passion—whether it's seafood, cycling, birdwatching, or bookshops—and trace it across the map. Be bold. Get off the main highways. Let your trip be less about *getting somewhere* and more about *getting something* out of it. Connection. Curiosity. Clarity.

So here's the big question: **What do you want this trip to mean?** Are you looking to disconnect from the chaos, or reconnect with someone you love? Do you want to relive history, or make some of your own? This isn't just about seeing Maryland—it's about *experiencing it*, one carefully chosen mile at a time.

BUDGETING YOUR MARYLAND RV ADVENTURE

Stretching Your Dollars Without Shrinking the Experience

Let me tell you a secret most RVers don't share out loud: It's not the price of the RV that gets you—it's everything else. The first time we took a "budget-friendly" road trip through Maryland, I thought we were being careful. We packed our own food, skipped the souvenir shops, and stayed in state parks instead of fancy resorts. But halfway through the trip, I checked our bank account and had that gut-punch moment—*Where did all the money go?*

Have you ever had that creeping feeling that maybe your dream trip is costing you more than it should? That maybe you're doing something wrong—or worse, that this whole freedom-on-the-road thing is only for people with deep pockets? I've been there. And I want to tell you something true: **RV travel can be affordable—but only if you understand where your money's going and how to make smarter choices at every stop.**

This chapter is your wallet's best friend. I'm going to walk you through exactly what to expect in terms of RV costs across Maryland—from campground fees to fuel, from park passes to sneaky extras. I'll also give you the inside scoop on discounts, free camping spots, and the off-season magic that most people overlook. Maryland is one of the best states in the U.S. for low-cost adventures—**if you know how to travel it right.**

The Real Costs of RVing in Maryland: What to Expect

Let's break down the most common RV expenses you'll encounter in Maryland:

1. Campground Fees

State Parks: Expect to pay $25–$40 per night. Sites with electric hookups average $35. Examples: Greenbrier State Park, Assateague State Park.

Private Campgrounds & RV Resorts: These range from $45 to $100+ per night, depending on location and amenities. Expect the higher end near Ocean City and Annapolis.

County & Municipal Parks: Often overlooked gems. $15–$30 per night, sometimes with water/electric. Spots like Tuckahoe or Patapsco Valley are budget gold.

Boondocking (Free or Low-Cost Dry Camping): Harder to find in Maryland but possible in certain forest areas, visitor centers, or large retail parking lots (with permission).

2. Fuel Costs

Maryland's average gas price hovers around **$3.20–$3.60/gallon**, depending on region and season. With most RVs getting **8–12 MPG**, you're looking at:

$60–$100 for a full tank

$0.30–$0.45 per mile driven

Pro tip: **Eastern Shore routes are flatter and more fuel-efficient** than mountain drives in Western Maryland.

3. Entry Fees & Passes

State Parks: Typically $3–$5 per person or per vehicle for day use. Campers often covered.

National Parks & Historic Sites: Antietam, Catoctin Mountain Park, Fort McHenry may charge $10–$20 per vehicle or offer free days.

Annual Passes: Maryland Park Service Passport ($75/year) gets you free day-use entry for every state park—worth it for longer trips.

4. Tolls & Bridges

The **Chesapeake Bay Bridge (US-50)** charges $4–$6 for cars, more for RVs with multiple axles.

EZ-Pass discounts help—get one if you're doing multiple crossings or driving I-95.

Money-Saving Tips That Actually Work

1. Travel Off-Peak Peak travel season in Maryland is **June to August**, especially near the beach. But spring and fall? **Milder weather, fewer crowds, and lower rates.** You'll save 20–30% on campground fees and find last-minute availability. Fall foliage in the mountains is *priceless—and practically free.*

2. Use Camping Memberships

Harvest Hosts: $99/year to stay overnight at farms, wineries, and breweries—many across Maryland.

Boondockers Welcome: Like couchsurfing for RVs. Friendly hosts, free stays.

Passport America: 50% off thousands of campgrounds. Several participating in Maryland.

Good Sam & KOA: Offer discounts and campground perks, especially near tourist areas.

3. Look for Free Activities & Hidden Deals

Maryland is full of **free-access nature preserves**, **walking tours**, **museums with donation-based entries**, and **low-cost festivals**.

Free ranger-led hikes at places like Sugarloaf Mountain and Gunpowder Falls.

Free entry days at historic sites (check NPS calendar).

Annapolis and Frederick often host open-air concerts, food events, and art walks with no entry fee.

4. Shop Smart, Eat Smart

Stock up at **local farmers markets**—cheaper and fresher than supermarkets.

Cook in your RV kitchen to save big. Even one meal out per day can blow your budget.

Plan picnic stops: many scenic parks have free grills and seating areas with million-dollar views.

5. Track Every Dollar (Yes, Every One)

Use a simple app like **RV Life**, **Roadtrippers Plus**, or even **Google Sheets** to log your spending in real-time. You'd be amazed how quickly small purchases add up: ice, firewood, forgotten chargers, last-minute snacks at gas stations. **Knowledge is power, and power saves money.**

Free & Nearly-Free Maryland Adventures You Don't Want to Miss

Assateague Island National Seashore (Off-Peak): Camp for under $30 and walk the beach with wild horses.

Swallow Falls State Park: $3 entry gets you access to one of the most stunning waterfall hikes in the Mid-Atlantic.

Harriet Tubman Underground Railroad Scenic Byway: Self-guided drive with no cost and deep emotional impact.

C&O Canal Towpath: Hike, bike, or paddle—all for free.

Baltimore's Inner Harbor on a Budget: Skip the pricey attractions. Walk the waterfront, tour historic ships on discounted days, and visit museums on free-admission nights.

More Adventure, Less Overhead

Here's what I wish someone had told me before my first RV trip through Maryland: **Your experience doesn't need to cost a fortune to be unforgettable.** In fact, the memories that stick with me aren't the ones where we splurged—they're the ones where we slowed down, found a quiet overlook, roasted marshmallows under the stars, and didn't spend a dime doing it. So ask yourself: **What do you really need to feel rich on the road?** Maybe it's not five-star amenities or daily excursions. Maybe it's space to breathe. Time to reconnect. Sunsets you didn't plan for, and stories you couldn't have made up. With a bit of planning and some insider knowledge, you can explore every inch of Maryland's wild coastlines, scenic mountains, and historic towns—**without breaking the bank.** Let your budget work for you, not against you. Let it shape a trip that's thoughtful, meaningful, and deeply yours.

CHAPTER 2

MARYLAND'S SCENIC ROUTES AND HIGHWAYS

THE CHESAPEAKE COUNTRY SCENIC BYWAY

Have you ever felt the pull of the open road, the allure of the horizon, and the promise of discovery? I have. And it was on the Chesapeake Country Scenic Byway that I found a journey not just through landscapes, but through time, culture, and the very soul of the Chesapeake Bay. This chapter is an invitation to share that journey with you—a journey that winds through picturesque towns, historic sites, and serene waterscapes, offering a tapestry of experiences that are as enriching as they are unforgettable.

The Allure of the Chesapeake Country Scenic Byway

The Chesapeake Country Scenic Byway isn't just a road; it's a story unfolding with every mile. Stretching over 200 miles through Maryland's Eastern Shore, it meanders along the western shore of the Chesapeake Bay, connecting a series of charming towns, historic sites, and natural wonders. As you drive, the landscape shifts from bustling towns to tranquil waters, from rich history to vibrant culture, each turn offering a new chapter in this living narrative. But what makes this byway truly captivating isn't just the scenery—it's the stories embedded in every corner. It's the legacy of the watermen who have harvested the bay's bounty for generations. It's the colonial architecture that whispers tales of a bygone era. It's the communities that have thrived along these shores, each with its unique character and charm.

St. Michaels: A Maritime Gem

St. Michaels Map

My journey began in St. Michaels, a town that feels like a step back in time. Known as the "Town That Fooled the British" during the War of 1812, St. Michaels boasts a rich maritime heritage. The Chesapeake Bay Maritime Museum is a must-visit, offering a hands-on experience with the region's boating history. As I wandered through the exhibits, I could almost hear the creak of wooden ships and the call of seagulls overhead. Dining in St. Michaels is a treat for the senses. The Crab Claw Restaurant, perched on the water's edge, serves up some of the freshest crab cakes I've ever tasted. The sweet, tender meat paired with a tangy mustard sauce was a culinary delight that still lingers in my memory.

Cambridge: Where History Meets Nature

Continuing south, I arrived in Cambridge, a town where history and nature coexist harmoniously. The Harriet Tubman Museum and Educational Center offers a poignant glimpse into the life of the legendary abolitionist. Walking through the exhibits, I was moved by the courage and determination that defined Tubman's life. Just outside the town lies the Blackwater National Wildlife Refuge, a haven for birdwatchers and nature enthusiasts. I spent hours hiking the trails, spotting bald eagles and other wildlife in their natural habitat. The tranquility of the refuge provided a perfect counterbalance to the historical intensity of the museum.

Rock Hall: The Pearl of the Chesapeake

Rock Hall, often referred to as the "Pearl of the Chesapeake," was a delightful surprise. This small town exudes a laid-back charm that invites relaxation. I spent my days exploring the local shops and enjoying fresh seafood at local eateries. The evenings were reserved for watching the sunset over the bay—a spectacle that never failed to captivate.

Chestertown: A Step into Colonial America

Chestertown offered a fascinating glimpse into colonial America. The historic district is a treasure trove of 18th-century architecture, with red-brick sidewalks and colonial-era buildings lining the streets. I visited the Schooner Sultana, a replica of an 18th-century schooner, and learned about the region's maritime history. The town's vibrant arts scene added a contemporary flair to its historic charm. Galleries and artisan shops showcased local talent, and I found myself spending hours browsing the unique creations.

Easton: A Blend of Elegance and Charm

Easton was a blend of elegance and charm. The town's Victorian architecture and tree-lined streets create an inviting atmosphere. I visited the Academy Art Museum, which houses an impressive collection of American and European art. The museum's serene gardens provided a peaceful retreat after a day of exploration. Dining in Easton was a culinary adventure. I dined at several local restaurants, each offering a unique take on Chesapeake cuisine. From fresh seafood to innovative dishes, the dining experiences were as varied as they were delicious.

Cambridge: A Return to Tranquility

Returning to Cambridge towards the end of my journey, I found a renewed sense of tranquility. The town's historic charm and natural beauty had left a lasting impression. I spent my final days revisiting favorite spots and reflecting on the experiences that had made this journey unforgettable.

RV Campgrounds: Staying Close to Nature

For those traveling by RV, the Chesapeake Country Scenic Byway offers several campgrounds that provide proximity to the water and local attractions. Here are a few notable options: Janes Island State Park: Located near Crisfield, this park offers more than 2,900 acres of saltmarsh, 30 miles of water trails, and 103 campsites. It's a perfect base for exploring the surrounding area and enjoying water-based activities. Elk Neck State Park: Situated on a 100-foot bluff overlooking the Upper Chesapeake Bay, this park offers over 250 campsites, rustic cabins, and access to hiking trails and water recreation activities. Terrapin Nature Park: Near Stevensville, this park features a 3.25-mile oyster shell walking trail through wildflower meadows, wetlands, and sandy shorelines, offering scenic views of the Chesapeake Bay.

Dining Delights Along the Byway

No journey along the Chesapeake Country Scenic Byway would be complete without indulging in the local cuisine. From fresh seafood to regional specialties, the towns along the route offer a variety of dining experiences: The Crab Claw Restaurant (St. Michaels): Known for its famous crab cakes and waterfront dining. Blue Ruin (Cambridge): A local favorite offering regional dishes like J.M. Clayton lump crab. Lighthouse Restaurant and Dockbar (Solomons Island): Offers delicious Chesapeake Bay cuisine with views of the water. The Red Roost (Chesapeake Beach): A crab house established in 1974, offering a variety of seafood dishes.

Reflections on the Journey

Reflecting on my journey along the Chesapeake Country Scenic Byway, I realize that it was more than just a road trip—it was an immersion into the heart of the Chesapeake Bay region. Each town, each stop, offered a unique experience that contributed to a deeper understanding and appreciation of this beautiful area. Whether you're a history buff, nature enthusiast, or culinary adventurer, the Chesapeake Country Scenic Byway offers something for everyone. It's a journey that invites you to slow down, explore, and connect with the rich tapestry of life along the Chesapeake Bay.

THE NATIONAL ROAD (U.S. ROUTE 40)

Have you ever driven a road that feels like a living testament to history? A road that whispers tales of pioneers, soldiers, and travelers who journeyed before you? U.S. Route 40, known as the National Road, is one such path. As one of America's oldest highways, it stretches across Maryland, offering a rich tapestry of historical landmarks, scenic vistas, and charming towns. In this chapter, we'll embark on a journey along this historic route, exploring its significance, the towns it connects, and the experiences that await travelers.

The Legacy of the National Road

The National Road was America's first federally funded interstate highway, commissioned in 1806 to facilitate westward expansion. Stretching from Baltimore, Maryland, to Vandalia, Illinois, it played a pivotal role in the nation's development. In Maryland, the road traverses through the Appalachian Mountains, connecting various towns and offering travelers a glimpse into the past.

Driving along this route is like flipping through the pages of a history book. From the cobblestone streets of historic towns to the remnants of 19th-century inns and taverns, every mile tells a story. The road itself, with its winding paths and scenic overlooks, offers more than just a drive—it offers a journey through time.

Frederick: A Blend of History and Modern Charm

Our journey begins in Frederick, a city that beautifully blends its rich history with modern attractions. Founded in 1745, Frederick boasts a historic downtown filled with preserved 18th and 19th-century architecture. As you stroll through the streets, you'll encounter charming boutiques, art galleries, and cafes housed in historic buildings.

One of the city's highlights is the National Museum of Civil War Medicine, which offers an in-depth look at medical practices during the Civil War. Nearby, the Schifferstadt Architectural Museum provides insights into early German-American architecture.

For dining, Frederick offers a plethora of options. From farm-to-table restaurants to international cuisines, there's something to satisfy every palate. Don't miss the local breweries that offer unique craft beers brewed with local ingredients.

Hagerstown: Gateway to the West

Continuing westward, we reach Hagerstown, a city that served as a gateway for westward travelers in the 19th century. The Hager House, built in 1740 by the city's founder, Jonathan Hager, offers a glimpse into colonial life. Located in Hagerstown City Park, the house is surrounded by beautiful landscapes and is a perfect spot for a picnic.

Hagerstown's historic district is a treasure trove of 19th-century architecture. The Jonathan Hager House and Museum, located in City Park, offers guided tours that delve into the city's early history. The nearby Washington County Museum of Fine Arts showcases a diverse collection of art, including works by the Old Masters and American artists.

For those interested in local cuisine, Hagerstown offers a variety of dining options. From traditional American fare to international dishes, the city's restaurants cater to diverse tastes. Don't forget to explore the local farmers' markets for fresh produce and artisanal goods.

Sharpsburg and Antietam National Battlefield: A Step Back in Time

A short drive from Hagerstown brings us to Sharpsburg, home to the Antietam National Battlefield. The site of the bloodiest single-day battle in American history, Antietam offers visitors a chance to reflect on the nation's past. The battlefield is preserved as a national park, with monuments, walking trails, and a visitor center that provides educational exhibits.

The Pry House Field Hospital Museum, located on the battlefield, offers insights into Civil War-era medical practices. The museum is housed in the former headquarters of Union General George McClellan and provides a unique perspective on the war's impact on soldiers and civilians alike.

Hancock: A Quaint Canal Town

Further west, we arrive in Hancock, a small town that offers a peaceful respite for travelers. Located along the Chesapeake and Ohio Canal, Hancock is a haven for history enthusiasts and nature lovers. The town's Visitor Center, housed in a historic canal home, provides information about the canal's history and the town's role in the National Road's development.

Nearby, the Blue Goose Bakery offers delicious baked goods, perfect for a mid-journey snack. The town also features antique shops and local eateries that provide a taste of small-town charm.

Williamsport: A Canal Town with Rich History

Just a short drive from Hancock is Williamsport, another canal town that offers a glimpse into the past. The town's Visitor Center, located in a historic building, provides information about the Chesapeake and Ohio Canal and its significance to the National Road.

One of Williamsport's unique attractions is the restored canal boat ride over a 1900s-era aqueduct. Visitors can experience what it was like to travel the canal in the early 20th century. The town also features a working lock and lockkeeper's house, offering demonstrations of how the canal operated.

Antietam Entertainment & Dinner Theater: A Cultural Experience

Located near Funkstown, the Antietam Entertainment & Dinner Theater offers a unique blend of live performances and dining. The theater hosts a variety of shows throughout the year, including musicals, comedies, and dramas. The dinner theater experience allows guests to enjoy a meal while watching a live performance, making for a memorable evening.

RV-Friendly Stops Along the National Road

For travelers journeying along the National Road in RVs, several campgrounds offer convenient and scenic accommodations:

Hagerstown / Antietam Battlefield KOA Holiday: Located in Williamsport, this campground offers amenities such as a swimming pool, fishing opportunities, and a diner serving classic American fare. The campground's proximity to Antietam National Battlefield makes it an ideal base for exploring the area.

Cumberland KOA: Situated in the western part of Maryland, this campground offers spacious sites, hiking trails, and a pet-friendly environment. It's a great spot for those looking to explore the Allegheny Mountains and the historic town of Cumberland.

Green Ridge State Forest Campground: Located near Flintstone, this campground offers a more rustic experience with hiking trails, fishing spots, and opportunities for wildlife viewing. It's perfect for nature enthusiasts seeking solitude.

Dining Delights Along the National Road

No journey along the National Road would be complete without sampling the local cuisine. Here are some dining establishments worth stopping for:

Dan's Restaurant & Tap House (Boonsboro): Known for its hearty American fare and wide selection of craft beers, Dan's offers a cozy atmosphere perfect for a meal after a day of exploring.

The Bavarian Inn (Shepherdstown): Offering authentic German cuisine and stunning views of the Potomac River, The Bavarian Inn provides a picturesque setting for a meal.

The Trolley Stop (Ellicott City): A historic restaurant serving classic American dishes, The Trolley Stop offers a charming atmosphere and a menu filled with favorites.

THE APPALACHIAN MOUNTAINS SCENIC BYWAY

Have you ever yearned for a drive that takes you away from the everyday noise, immersing you in the majesty of nature's untouched beauty? That was exactly how I felt the first time I ventured onto Maryland's Appalachian Mountains Scenic Byway. The air smelled fresher, the landscapes soared higher, and each mile seemed to unravel a secret hiding just beyond the next bend. This route isn't just a road; it's a soul-stirring escape into the heart of Maryland's western wilderness, where mountains, forests, and history entwine to create a breathtaking experience.

Discovering the Appalachian Mountains Scenic Byway

Stretching across the western edge of Maryland, the Appalachian Mountains Scenic Byway guides travelers through some of the most spectacular mountain vistas in the state. This route is part of a larger network that follows the Appalachian range stretching from Georgia to Maine, but Maryland's section offers a unique charm—a blend of rugged wilderness, charming small towns, and tranquil parks. Driving here, I was struck by how every turn unveiled panoramic views of rolling ridges, dense hardwood forests, and crystal-clear streams. The road itself is a winding masterpiece, hugging mountain contours and inviting you to slow down and savor the journey.

Hiking and Exploration: The Appalachian Trail and Beyond

One of the true highlights along this scenic byway is its proximity to the legendary Appalachian Trail. Whether you're a seasoned hiker or just someone who loves to breathe in the fresh mountain air on a short walk, the trailhead access points along the byway are perfect gateways to adventure. I recall stepping onto the trail near Pen Mar Park, feeling both humbled and exhilarated by the vastness of the forest and the promise of discovery just ahead. The trail here offers sections that vary from gentle strolls to challenging ascents, ensuring that every adventurer finds their pace. Nearby, Catoctin Mountain Park offers another treasure trove of natural beauty and history. This national park is famed for its dense forests, wildlife sightings, and crystal-clear streams. The park's diverse hiking trails range from easy nature walks to strenuous climbs, all framed by the stunning backdrop of the Appalachian foothills. I spent an unforgettable afternoon here, hiking to the summit of Chimney Rock—a vantage point that rewards you with sweeping views of the valley below. Just a bit further west lies Rocky Gap State Park, a hidden gem with a serene lake, well-maintained trails, and a challenging golf course. The park's lake is perfect for kayaking and fishing, while the hiking trails offer peaceful walks that weave through dense forests and around rugged cliffs. The fresh mountain air and soothing sounds of nature made this one of my favorite stops along the byway.

Small Town Charm: Mountain Communities Along the Route

Traveling the Appalachian Mountains Scenic Byway also means encountering charming small towns where the pace slows and the community spirit shines. Towns like Frostburg and Cumberland offer a blend of history, culture, and hospitality that perfectly complement the natural beauty surrounding them. I loved strolling through Frostburg's historic downtown, with its inviting cafes, quirky shops, and friendly locals who were always ready to share a story or recommend a hidden hiking spot. Cumberland, known as the "Queen City," offers historic sites, art galleries, and the C&O Canal National Historical Park, where you can bike or walk along the scenic towpath.

RV Camping: Embracing the Mountain Wilderness

For those traveling by RV, the Appalachian Mountains Scenic Byway offers exceptional camping options that put you right in the heart of the wilderness. Here are some of the best RV-friendly campgrounds I discovered: Green Ridge State Forest Campground. Nestled within Maryland's largest contiguous forest, this campground offers rustic sites surrounded by towering trees, with miles of hiking and biking trails nearby. It's a perfect spot for adventurers seeking solitude and immersion in nature. Rocky Gap State Park Campground: Located along the scenic lake, this campground offers full hookups and modern amenities, making it ideal for families and those who prefer comfort without sacrificing proximity to nature. C&O Canal National Historical Park Campgrounds: Near Cumberland, several campgrounds provide access to the historic canal trail, perfect for those wanting to explore by bike or on foot during the day. Camping here isn't just about parking your RV; it's about waking up to misty mountain mornings, the scent of pine in the air, and the peaceful chorus of birdsong—a genuine chance to disconnect and recharge.

Dining and Local Flavor

No mountain adventure is complete without savoring the local flavors. Along the byway, small-town diners and family-run restaurants serve hearty meals that fuel your explorations. I highly recommend stopping at the Frostburg Depot Restaurant, where you can indulge in classic comfort food after a long day of hiking. Their homemade soups and fresh-baked pies are legendary. In Cumberland, The Crabby Pig offers a delicious mix of barbecue and Chesapeake Bay seafood, perfect for those craving a taste of local tradition.

Reflections on the Appalachian Mountains Scenic Byway

Reflecting on my journey along the Appalachian Mountains Scenic Byway, I'm reminded that this route is more than a drive—it's a sensory experience that awakens your love for nature and history. The blend of mountain vistas, hiking trails, small-town warmth, and serene camping spots creates an adventure that stays with you long after the trip ends. Whether you're seeking thrilling outdoor activities or peaceful moments surrounded by towering trees, this byway offers an authentic slice of Maryland's wild heart.

CHAPTER 3

BEST CAMPGROUNDS AND RV PARKS IN MARYLAND

THE UNFORGETTABLE QUEST FOR THE PERFECT MARYLAND CAMPGROUND

Have you ever felt that magnetic pull to escape the chaos of everyday life, to disconnect from the noise, and breathe in the sweet, crisp air of the wilderness? That's exactly what I felt the first time I hit the road in my RV, chasing the promise of peaceful nights under vast star-studded skies and mornings painted in golden sunlight. But finding the perfect spot—where nature's beauty meets practical comfort—was a quest filled with both thrilling discoveries and frustrating dead ends.

Maryland, often overshadowed by its bigger neighbors, harbors some of the most stunning and thoughtfully equipped campgrounds for RV travelers. It's a state where lush forests, winding rivers, and rolling hills converge, creating a playground for adventure seekers and peace lovers alike. But with so many options, how do you pick the campground that truly fits your vibe?

If you've ever wondered what makes a campground more than just a place to park your RV—what transforms it into a sanctuary for the soul—this chapter is your treasure map. I'm going to share the secrets of Maryland's top state parks perfect for RV campers, sprinkled with my personal tales of joyous mornings, unexpected challenges, and hard-earned lessons. Along the way, I'll arm you with insider tips to snag those coveted spots during peak seasons, and strategies to maximize your outdoor experience without compromise.

Ready to embark on a journey to Maryland's best campgrounds? Let's dive in.

Section 1: The Magic of Maryland's State Parks for RV Campers

Why Maryland?

Maryland might be small in size, but its natural diversity and welcoming parks make it a powerhouse for camping enthusiasts. From the Chesapeake Bay's shimmering shores to the Appalachian foothills, this state offers a spectrum of ecosystems that transform every camping trip into a unique adventure.

But what truly sets Maryland apart? For me, it was the sense of balance. Not too remote to feel isolated, yet far enough from city bustle to immerse in nature's tranquility. Every campground I visited held something special—a promise of breathtaking sunsets, star-filled nights, and fresh morning air that felt like a reset button for my soul.

The Unique Appeal of RV Camping in Maryland

RV camping brings a special flavor to the outdoor experience: it's about comfort meeting adventure. The right campground must offer not only stunning scenery but practical amenities like electric hookups, dump stations, and reliable water sources. Maryland's state parks understand this delicate dance, ensuring their facilities serve both rugged explorers and those seeking a cozy home on wheels.

Think about it—have you ever rolled into a campground only to find overcrowded sites, sketchy hookups, or a vibe that just doesn't resonate? It can turn your dream escape into a stress-filled scramble. But Maryland's best parks? They've got that balance nailed down.

Section 2: Top Maryland State Parks for RV Campers

Greenbrier State Park: The Classic Camper's Haven

Nestled near the South Mountain Range, Greenbrier State Park was the first place where I truly felt what RV camping in Maryland could be. The air was thick with the scent of pine and damp earth, and the tranquil Greenbrier Lake beckoned for early morning kayaking.

What makes Greenbrier special?

Spacious campsites: Many sites offer level gravel pads with 30/50 amp electric hookups and water access.

Amenities: Clean restrooms, modern shower facilities, and a convenient dump station.

Activities: Swimming, hiking, fishing, and even a playground for families.

Pro tip: Book early, especially for weekend stays in summer. Sites fill up fast, and the best ones—those lakeside gems—are snapped up within weeks. I once missed out on my favorite spot because I waited too long, and trust me, the disappointment stings.

Patapsco Valley State Park: Where Rivers Meet Forests

This sprawling park, hugging the Patapsco River, offers over 16,000 acres of forest and trail magic. RV campers love it for the sense of seclusion despite its proximity to Baltimore.

Highlights:

Multiple campgrounds with full hookups.

Extensive hiking and biking trails, including the famous Grist Mill Trail.

Rich history with preserved mill ruins scattered along the river.

The first time I camped here, the gentle rush of the river was my lullaby, and waking up to the sound of birds felt like a gentle nudge to embrace the day.

However, the park's popularity means you must plan your trip around less busy times—mid-week stays offer more quiet and space.

Elk Neck State Park: The Coastal Charm

If you're craving a waterfront experience, Elk Neck State Park is a must. Located on the Chesapeake Bay's edge, this park blends forested beauty with stunning water views.

Why I keep coming back:

Sites with electric and water hookups nestled among towering hardwoods.

Easy access to the beach and boating facilities.

Breathtaking sunsets over the bay.

Booking here requires timing savvy. Summer weekends can be fully booked months ahead. Consider shoulder seasons—late spring or early fall—for a quieter, more personal experience.

Section 3: Insider Tips for Booking and Enjoying Maryland RV Campgrounds

Timing Is Everything

Have you ever planned a camping trip only to find your chosen park fully booked? I've been there, standing at the entrance gate with nowhere to park and nowhere else to go. Maryland's most popular parks fill quickly, especially between May and September.

Strategy:

Reserve as early as possible—most Maryland state parks accept bookings up to six months ahead.

Avoid weekends if you crave solitude; weekdays or off-season months like April or October can offer a peaceful alternative.

Consider holiday weekends carefully—expect crowds and limited availability.

Choosing the Right Site for Your RV

Not all campsites are created equal. Some are better suited for big rigs; others are cozy spots perfect for smaller RVs or camper vans.

Things to look for:

Length and width of the site: Make sure your rig fits comfortably without blocking roadways.

Hookups: Determine if you need 30 amp or 50 amp electric, water, and sewer connections.

Terrain: Gravel pads are ideal for stability; avoid overly sloped or rocky areas.

Shade and privacy: Sites shaded by trees provide cooler spots and a sense of seclusion.

I once learned the hard way by parking in a too-tight site, waking up with my camper tilting uncomfortably. Lesson learned—always check site dimensions before booking.

Packing and Preparation Tips

Maryland's weather can be unpredictable, shifting from hot summer days to chilly nights rapidly. Packing smart can make or break your trip.

Essentials to pack:

Layered clothing for temperature swings.

Mosquito and tick repellent— especially near wooded areas.

Backup power options (solar panels or generators) for longer stays.

Outdoor gear for hiking, fishing, and water activities.

Section 4: Real Stories from the Road

(Here, weave in personal anecdotes about memorable camping experiences, challenges faced—such as weather changes, wildlife encounters, or site mishaps—and how these moments shaped your understanding and love for Maryland's campgrounds.)

Section 5: Beyond the Campsites — Exploring Maryland's Surroundings

While the campgrounds provide a home base, Maryland's rich culture, history, and natural beauty extend beyond your RV door.

Explore nearby hiking trails and waterfalls.

Visit charming small towns and historic sites.

Sample local food and craft brews after a day outdoors.

Your Maryland RV Adventure Awaits

Have you felt that irresistible tug to plan your own Maryland RV getaway? These state parks offer more than just a place to park—they offer a chance to reconnect with nature, challenge yourself, and create unforgettable memories.

So, what's stopping you? Pack your bags, fire up the engine, and let Maryland's campgrounds welcome you home.

LUXURY RV RESORTS AND GLAMPING SITES: ELEVATE YOUR MARYLAND CAMPING EXPERIENCE

The Allure of Luxury on the Road

Have you ever dreamed of camping, but with a touch of indulgence? The kind of trip where you don't just survive in the wilderness—you thrive in it, surrounded by upscale amenities that make your adventure feel like a five-star retreat?

I remember the moment I discovered luxury RV resorts—it was like stepping into a whole new world. Gone were the days of worrying about hookups, cramped spaces, or limited facilities. Instead, I found myself lounging poolside after a morning hike, indulging in spa treatments, and even hitting the golf course—all just steps away from my spacious RV pad.

Maryland, despite its modest size, has embraced this trend beautifully. For travelers who crave nature's beauty but refuse to sacrifice comfort, the state offers an enticing lineup of high-end RV resorts and glamping sites. Here, you get the best of both worlds: the breathtaking landscapes of the Mid-Atlantic region coupled with the luxury and convenience that turn every moment into a mini-vacation.

Yogi Bear's Jellystone Park™ in Williamsport: Family-Friendly Fun Meets Comfort

When I first rolled into Yogi Bear's Jellystone Park™ in Williamsport, I wasn't quite sure what to expect. I'd heard about it being family-friendly, but what really surprised me was the sheer range of amenities designed to delight every age group.

Imagine a campground with a sparkling swimming pool, splash pads, mini-golf, and even a dedicated arcade—all within walking distance of your RV site. The sites themselves are roomy, with full hookups including 50 amp electric, water, and sewer, and flat, well-maintained pads that made setting up a breeze.

What I loved most? The vibe. It's vibrant, fun, and filled with opportunities to meet fellow travelers, all while enjoying the comforts of home. Whether you're a family with kids or a couple looking for a lively, luxurious camping experience, Jellystone Park delivers.

Insider tip: Book well in advance during holiday weekends; the demand here is high, especially in summer. Also, try to snag a site near the amenities for quick access, but if you prefer quiet, request sites on the park's periphery.

Chesapeake Bay RV Resort: Serenity and Sophistication on the Water

If your ideal luxury getaway involves stunning waterfront views and tranquil surroundings, Chesapeake Bay RV Resort is a dream come true. Nestled along the Chesapeake Bay, this resort combines the peaceful beauty of the water with high-end RV accommodations and resort-style facilities.

The first time I stayed here, I was blown away by the spaciousness of the sites—wide, level, and outfitted with full hookups and cable TV access. The resort features a swimming pool, clubhouse, fitness center, and even kayak rentals, allowing guests to explore the bay at their own pace.

What struck me most was the attention to detail—from impeccably maintained grounds to friendly staff who genuinely cared about the guest experience. Here, luxury isn't just about the amenities; it's about the feeling of being pampered in a serene natural setting.

Glamping: Embracing Nature Without Sacrificing Comfort

Let's face it—sometimes, the idea of setting up a tent or maneuvering an RV feels overwhelming, especially if you're new to camping or just craving a hassle-free way to enjoy the outdoors. That's where glamping steps in—a perfect middle ground that lets you soak in nature's wonders without giving up the luxuries you love.

Maryland offers a growing number of glamping sites that feature cozy yurts, safari tents, and fully furnished cabins equipped with plush beds, heating and cooling, and private decks. Imagine waking up to birdsong, stepping out onto a deck with a fresh cup of coffee in hand, and breathing in the crisp forest air—all without the fuss of pitching a tent.

During one glamping weekend at a site near Deep Creek Lake, I felt a profound sense of relaxation and connection. The experience reignited my love for nature while reminding me that comfort can coexist with adventure.

Pro tip: If you're considering glamping, check the site's amenities carefully—some offer full kitchens and bathrooms, while others keep things more rustic. This ensures you get exactly the experience you want.

Reflect and Imagine

Have you ever wondered what your perfect outdoor escape looks like? Is it a lively resort with pools and activities, or a quiet, elegant cabin nestled in the woods? Maybe it's a blend of both?

Luxury RV resorts and glamping sites in Maryland invite you to redefine camping on your own terms. They remind us that nature doesn't have to mean compromise, and adventure can be wrapped in comfort.

HIDDEN GEM CAMPGROUNDS AND SECLUDED ESCAPES: FIND YOUR PEACE OFF THE BEATEN PATH

The Quiet Call of Solitude

Have you ever yearned for a camping experience that feels like a secret whispered just for you? A place where the only sounds are rustling leaves, distant birdcalls, and the gentle ripple of a nearby river—far from the hum of busy campgrounds and the glow of city lights?

For me, these hidden gems in Maryland became a sanctuary when the noise of the world felt overwhelming. I craved solitude, a chance to truly unplug and reconnect with the essence of nature. The crowded, flashy campgrounds were fun for a while, but nothing compared to the peaceful magic of these secluded spots.

What if I told you that Maryland holds dozens of such quiet escapes—small, tucked-away campgrounds and RV parks where privacy is the norm and nature takes center stage?

Discovering Maryland's Hidden Treasures

The beauty of Maryland lies not just in its well-known parks, but in its lesser-explored corners. These off-the-radar campgrounds are nestled near calm riversides, tucked deep in forests, or perched on the outskirts of charming small towns. They offer a level of tranquility rare to find and a chance to slow down and breathe.

Quiet Riversides: Campgrounds Where Water Whispers

One of my favorite hidden escapes was a small, family-run campground along the banks of the Potomac River. The site wasn't marked on most maps, and cell service was patchy at best—a blessing for those craving digital detox. The sound of the flowing river at night lulled me to sleep, and waking up to mist hovering over the water felt like stepping into a dream.

If you're searching for similar serene riverside campgrounds, consider exploring areas around:

Potomac River State Forest — Offering primitive camping with some RV-friendly sites, this area is perfect for quiet reflection, fishing, and hiking.

Potomac River State Forest

Deep Creek Lake's quieter coves — Away from the bustling main lakefront, these spots provide peaceful water views and private shorelines.

Secluded Forests: Nature's Private Retreats

Maryland's dense woodlands hide some of the most peaceful camping experiences. I recall setting up camp deep in a secluded section of Savage River State Forest, where my only neighbors were the towering pines and an occasional deer wandering through the clearing.

Here, the campsites are spread out, often primitive or with minimal amenities—ideal for those who truly want to unplug. The air feels cooler, the shadows longer, and the stars brighter.

For RV travelers seeking these retreats, smaller state forests and lesser-known county parks can be gold mines. Examples include:

Savage River State Forest

Big Run State Park — Tucked away in Garrett County, offering a small, quiet campground with easy access to hiking and fishing.

Small-Town Charm Meets Quiet Camping

For campers who appreciate a balance of nature and local culture, Maryland's quaint towns offer campgrounds that feel like home bases for exploration and relaxation.

One gem I found near the historic town of Berlin combined quiet, spacious RV sites with easy access to charming shops, local eateries, and festivals. There's something special about camping near communities that welcome you warmly, yet allow you to retreat into quiet solitude by day's end.

Consider campgrounds near:

Berlin, Maryland — Close to Assateague Island but with a slower pace and fewer crowds.

St. Mary's County — Known for historic sites and quiet waterfront camping options

Secluded RV Parks: Privacy and Peace

If your idea of escape includes the convenience of RV hookups but without the hustle and bustle, Maryland offers a handful of lesser-known RV parks where privacy is prioritized.

These parks often feature:

Spacious lots with natural barriers like trees or shrubs between sites.

Limited occupancy to reduce noise and traffic.

Easy access to hiking trails or natural attractions, yet removed from busy highways.

Some options worth exploring are:

Quiet Waters RV Park — Known for a serene setting and attentive management.

Mountain Vista Campground — Tucked in Western Maryland's hills, offering panoramic views and peaceful surroundings.

Tips for Finding and Enjoying Hidden Gems

Do your research: Smaller parks and primitive sites may not be heavily advertised online. Local tourism boards, camping forums, and word of mouth can be invaluable resources.

Prepare for fewer amenities: Many hidden gems favor rustic charm over luxury. Bring extra supplies and prepare for limited hookups or facilities.

Practice Leave No Trace: Secluded spots are often fragile ecosystems. Respect the environment by minimizing impact and packing out all trash.

Be flexible: Secluded camping often requires adaptability—changing plans if sites are full or weather turns. But the reward is worth it.

Reflect: What Does Your Ideal Quiet Escape Look Like?

Have you ever dreamed of a getaway where your only company is nature itself? Where you can hear the whispers of the wind, watch a solo heron skim across the water, and fall asleep without a single car horn blaring in the distance?

Maryland's hidden campgrounds and secluded escapes offer this rare chance—a place to heal, reflect, and truly experience the magic of the outdoors on your own terms.

CHAPTER 4

MARYLAND'S NATIONAL AND STATE PARKS

ASSATEAGUE ISLAND NATIONAL SEASHORE

A Personal Journey to Assateague Island

I remember the first time I set foot on Assateague Island—how the salty breeze instantly wrapped around me like a warm, welcoming hug. The endless stretch of white sand, the wild horses grazing freely, and the sound of crashing waves made me feel both exhilarated and humble. But it wasn't just the breathtaking scenery that captivated me; it was the raw, untamed spirit of the island that spoke to a part of me I didn't know needed healing.

Have you ever felt that yearning to escape the clutter of modern life, to disconnect, and truly reconnect with nature? Assateague is that escape—a sanctuary that whispers stories of resilience and freedom. But my first visit was far from perfect. Battling mosquitoes, figuring out the right camping gear, and getting lost while searching for the lighthouse tested my resolve. Yet, every challenge only deepened my appreciation for the island's wild beauty.

If you're reading this, chances are you're drawn to the allure of Assateague—whether for adventure, peace, or a new kind of discovery. Let's embark on this journey together. I'll share the highs and lows of my experience, along with practical tips to ensure your trip is as memorable and smooth as possible.

The Magic of Assateague Island

Imagine a place where wild horses roam freely, their manes tousled by the ocean wind, untouched beaches stretch as far as the eye can see, and vibrant marshlands teem with life. That's Assateague Island National Seashore—a unique barrier island straddling Maryland and Virginia, preserved as a sanctuary for both wildlife and visitors seeking a slice of raw nature.

Why is Assateague so captivating? Is it the mystery of the wild ponies whose origins remain partly shrouded in legend? Or perhaps the powerful contrast of fragile ecosystems—beaches, dunes, marshes—existing side by side? These elements evoke a sense of wonder and curiosity, pulling you in deeper with every step.

When was the last time you witnessed nature's untamed beauty so intimately that it left you breathless? Assateague offers that kind of experience—and much more.

The Wild Horses: Living Symbols of Freedom

The iconic wild horses are Assateague's heart and soul. Encountering these majestic creatures, you realize they embody resilience and freedom, surviving harsh storms and scarce resources year after year.

But did you know the horses here are not entirely feral descendants from shipwrecked Spanish horses? The truth is more complex and fascinating—these ponies have been cared for by humans while still maintaining their wild essence. Managing their population and health is a delicate balance that park authorities continuously strive to maintain.

During my visit, I recall one unforgettable morning when I quietly watched a small herd grazing at dawn. Their calm presence was almost meditative, and I found myself wondering: what can these wild horses teach us about living with grace amid adversity?

Camping on Assateague Island: Embrace the Wild

For those who crave immersion, camping on Assateague is an incomparable experience. The campgrounds here offer more than just a place to sleep—they are gateways to the island's soul.

Where to camp? The Maryland side of Assateague features several excellent campgrounds, each with unique appeal:

Assateague Island Campground: The primary site on the Maryland side, located near the bay, offers tent and RV camping with amenities like water, flush toilets, and a dump station.

Backcountry Camping: For true adventurers, the island allows primitive camping spots away from the main campgrounds—think peaceful solitude under the stars, but be prepared with everything you need.

Private RV Parks Nearby: If you prefer full hookups and more facilities, there are nearby RV parks on the mainland that serve as convenient bases for day trips to the island.

Camping here is an emotional rollercoaster—from the awe of waking up to ocean views to the frustration of battling sand in every crevice of your tent. But isn't that part of what makes it unforgettable?

Have you ever felt that delicate tension between comfort and raw nature when camping? Embracing that tension can lead to some of the most rewarding moments of your life.

Outdoor Activities: Exploring the Island's Wonders

Assateague Island is a playground for outdoor enthusiasts. Here are some of my top recommendations and personal favorites:

Beachcombing: Early mornings are perfect for searching the shores for shells, driftwood, and treasures left behind by the tide. It's a peaceful way to connect with the rhythm of the ocean.

Birdwatching: The island is a haven for birdlife, especially migratory species. I found my binoculars indispensable for spotting rare birds like the piping plover or the great blue heron.

Assateague Lighthouse: Climbing the lighthouse is a must. From the top, you get panoramic views that make the effort worthwhile. The lighthouse also has a rich history, which deepens your connection to the place.

Kayaking and Canoeing: Exploring the bay side by kayak brings a new perspective on the island's ecosystems and wildlife.

Have you ever lost yourself in a single activity so completely that hours felt like minutes? These experiences are the heartbeats of Assateague.

Practical Tips for Your Visit

To truly enjoy Assateague Island, preparation is key. Here are actionable tips I learned the hard way:

Pack for Bugs: Mosquitoes and biting flies can be relentless, especially at dawn and dusk. Bring insect repellent with DEET and wear protective clothing.

Check Tides: The island's beaches and marshlands shift dramatically with tides. Plan your activities around tide charts to avoid surprises.

Respect the Wildlife: Never approach or feed the wild horses. Keep a safe distance, both for your safety and theirs.

Book Campsites Early: Assateague is popular—reserve spots well in advance, especially during summer.

Bring Essentials: Water, sunscreen, layered clothing, and a first-aid kit are non-negotiable.

Stay Informed: Check the National Park Service website for current alerts or closures.

Have you ever overlooked a simple detail on a trip and paid the price? Learning from others' mistakes can save you a lot of hassle.

Reflection: What Assateague Taught Me

Assateague Island is more than just a destination—it's a mirror reflecting life's unpredictability and beauty. The island taught me about resilience, about letting go of control, and about finding peace in wild places.

As you plan your trip, I encourage you to think: what are you hoping to find on Assateague? Is it solitude? Adventure? A deeper connection with nature? When you answer these questions honestly, your journey becomes not just a visit, but a transformation.

CATOCTIN MOUNTAIN PARK

Catoctin Mountain Park

Discovering the Hidden Gem of Catoctin Mountain

The first time I ventured into Catoctin Mountain Park, I was seeking something that neither city streets nor crowded beaches could offer: raw, rugged wilderness fused with a quiet, historic mystique. I remember driving up the winding mountain roads, my heart pounding with anticipation. The scent of pine trees filled the air, and the distant chirping of birds promised a day unlike any other.

Have you ever felt that undeniable pull toward a place where nature feels untouched and every step invites discovery? Catoctin Mountain Park offers exactly that—a refuge where your soul can breathe freely amid towering trees and panoramic vistas.

But this park isn't just about the beauty of nature. It's also home to Camp David, the President's retreat, a symbol of peace amid the wild. That unique intersection of natural splendor and historic significance gave my visit a sense of reverence and wonder I didn't expect.

The Rugged Beauty of Catoctin: Trails, Wildlife, and Views

Catoctin Mountain Park is a treasure trove for anyone who loves hiking, wildlife watching, or simply soaking in sweeping mountain views. The terrain here is rugged and diverse—steep ridges, deep valleys, and dense forests that seem to whisper ancient secrets.

One of my favorite trails is the **Wolf Rock Trail**—a moderate hike leading to a rocky outcrop with breathtaking views of the valley below. I still recall the exhilaration of reaching the summit, the wind rushing past me, and the sun casting golden light over the distant mountains. That moment felt like a reward for every sweaty step and every aching muscle.

Have you ever experienced that pure, unfiltered joy of conquering a challenging trail? Catoctin delivers that experience in spades.

Wildlife here is abundant and often shy. Early morning hikes rewarded me with glimpses of white-tailed deer gracefully bounding through the underbrush and a variety of birds singing unseen in the treetops. If you're lucky, you might even spot a black bear in the distance—always a thrilling, humbling experience.

Camp David: A Historic Secret Within the Wilderness

Catoctin's story deepens with its connection to Camp David, the presidential retreat nestled within the park's boundaries. While visitors aren't allowed direct access to the camp, knowing that such a significant place of diplomacy and quiet reflection exists within these woods adds an intriguing layer to the park's atmosphere.

During my visit, I found myself reflecting on the contrast between the simplicity of the natural world around me and the complex decisions that have been made within Camp David's secure walls. It reminded me that nature and history are often intertwined in ways we don't immediately see.

Have you ever stood in a place where history and nature converge, feeling the weight of stories untold? Catoctin offers that unique experience quietly, almost humbly.

Camping Near Catoctin Mountain Park: Where to Stay for Adventure and Comfort

For those who want to immerse themselves fully, camping near Catoctin Mountain Park is the way to go. While the park itself offers rustic camping experiences, many visitors opt for nearby RV campgrounds that provide easy access to trails and local attractions.

Some top options include:

Catoctin Mountain Park Campground: Primitive and backcountry camping options are available inside the park for those who want to truly disconnect and sleep under the stars.

Local RV Parks Near Thurmont: Just a few miles from the park's entrance, these campgrounds offer full hookups, showers, and conveniences—perfect for families or those new to camping.

Private Campgrounds: Several private sites in the area provide amenities like Wi-Fi and laundry, great for longer stays or RV travelers seeking comfort without losing proximity to nature.

I learned the importance of booking early, especially in peak seasons. On my second visit, I arrived without a reservation and was forced to settle for a less ideal spot, which meant longer drives and less time on the trails—an experience I hope you avoid.

Best Trails and Activities: How to Make the Most of Your Visit

Catoctin Mountain Park offers something for every adventurer. Here are some must do activities and tips I gathered from experience:

Hiking: Besides Wolf Rock, try the **Louden Mountain Trail** and the **Cunningham Falls Trail** for diverse landscapes and stunning waterfalls.

Wildlife Watching: Dawn and dusk are prime times. Bring binoculars and a camera, but always maintain respectful distance.

Photography: The light filtering through the dense canopy in the early morning is magical—perfect for nature photography.

Picnicking: Several designated areas make for relaxing lunch spots surrounded by nature's tranquility.

Fishing and Boating: Nearby Cunningham Falls State Park offers fishing and paddle boating if you want a change of pace.

Have you ever felt so connected to the outdoors that time seems to slow? Catoctin's trails invite you to lose yourself—and find yourself all at once.

Practical Tips for Visiting Catoctin Mountain Park

From my experience, here are some essential tips to ensure your visit is enjoyable and safe:

Wear Proper Footwear: Trails can be rocky and steep.

Bring Plenty of Water and Snacks: Hydration and energy are crucial on longer hikes.

Check Weather Conditions: Mountain weather can change rapidly.

Respect Park Rules: Especially around Camp David boundaries and wildlife areas.

Plan Ahead: Download maps, and consider guided tours for deeper insights.

Leave No Trace: Preserve the park's beauty for future generations.

What Catoctin Taught Me About Nature and History

My time at Catoctin Mountain Park was more than just a hiking trip—it was a lesson in balance. The park's wild, untamed beauty sits alongside a place of peaceful diplomacy, reminding me that nature and human history are deeply connected.

I left with a renewed sense of respect for both the earth beneath my feet and the stories that shape our world. And I wonder, when you visit Catoctin, what lessons will it teach *you*? What moments will take your breath away, and which quiet corners will become your secret refuge?

CALVERT CLIFFS STATE PARK

A Journey Back Through Time at Calvert Cliffs

The moment I first laid eyes on the towering Calvert Cliffs, I was struck by a profound sense of awe—not just for their sheer natural beauty, but for the ancient story they silently tell. These rugged cliffs aren't just a spectacular geological formation; they are time machines carved in stone, holding fossils that date back millions of years.

Have you ever stood somewhere so steeped in history and wondered what secrets the earth beneath your feet might be hiding? Calvert Cliffs is that place—a remarkable intersection where nature's artistry and deep time converge in a breathtaking display.

My first fossil hunt here was nothing short of thrilling. I remember the excitement of spotting a tiny shark tooth embedded in the sand, holding a piece of a world that existed 10 million years ago. That discovery was a spark—a gateway to curiosity, wonder, and a deeper connection to nature than I'd ever experienced before.

The Cliffs: Nature's Majestic Time Capsules

Calvert Cliffs rise dramatically above the Chesapeake Bay shoreline, their red-brown face marked by the constant ebb and flow of tides and time. The cliffs are composed of sedimentary deposits from the Miocene epoch, offering a rare window into the prehistoric past.

Walking along the cliffs, you can't help but feel the power of erosion and natural forces at work—each fallen piece tells a story, and every fossil fragment is a chapter in Earth's vast history.

But the cliffs themselves are fragile, and visitors must respect protected areas to preserve this natural treasure for future generations. It's a delicate balance between exploration and conservation.

Fossil Hunting: Unearthing Ancient Treasures

One of the most exhilarating activities at Calvert Cliffs is fossil hunting along the beach. The shoreline is littered with remnants of prehistoric marine life—shark teeth, shells, and bones from creatures that once thrived in a warm, shallow sea.

I still remember the first fossil I found—a tiny, gleaming shark tooth no bigger than a fingernail. That moment felt like touching a secret passed down through millions of years. Have you ever experienced the thrill of discovery that connects you to a world so distant yet tangible?

If you're planning to hunt for fossils, here are some tips to maximize your success:

Visit during low tide: The beach reveals more fossils when the tide is out.

Bring a small shovel or digging tool: Gently sift through the sand near the base of the cliffs.

Wear sturdy water shoes: The shoreline can be rocky and slippery.

Use a bucket and mesh screen: To separate fossils from sand easily.

Check local regulations: Collecting fossils is permitted, but some areas are protected.

Remember, patience is key. Sometimes hours pass with little to show for it, but the moment you find a fossil, the wait becomes worth every second.

Trails and Wildlife: More Than Just Fossils

While the fossil-rich beach draws many visitors, Calvert Cliffs State Park offers much more than just paleontological wonders. The park features several hiking trails weaving through lush forests, wetlands, and alongside creeks teeming with life.

During one hike on the **Cliff Trail**, I encountered deer darting through the underbrush and spotted a rare Bald Eagle soaring overhead—a breathtaking sight that made my heart race. The combination of forest, water, and open bay views creates a rich habitat for birds, mammals, and amphibians.

Are you someone who finds joy in spotting a flash of wildlife in the wild? The variety here is astounding and will delight bird watchers, photographers, and nature lovers alike.

Camping and RV Options Near Calvert Cliffs

For visitors who want to extend their stay and dive deeper into the park's wonders, camping is an ideal choice. While Calvert Cliffs itself doesn't have an on-site RV campground, several excellent options lie nearby, offering easy access to the park's beaches and trails:

Flag Ponds Nature Park Campground: A short drive from Calvert Cliffs, this site offers both tent and RV camping with modern amenities.

Nearby Private Campgrounds: Several private parks in the region provide full hookups and family-friendly facilities, perfect for extended stays.

Chesapeake Bay Access: Many campgrounds are situated close enough to enjoy kayaking, fishing, or simply relaxing by the water after a day of hiking.

I learned that planning ahead is crucial, especially during summer weekends when campgrounds fill quickly. Reserving your spot early ensures you have a comfortable base for your adventures.

Practical Tips for Visiting Calvert Cliffs

Drawing from my visits, here are essential tips to make your trip smooth and rewarding:

Wear layered clothing: The weather can shift quickly near the bay.

Bring sunscreen and bug spray: The shoreline and forested areas attract mosquitoes.

Start early: Fossil hunting and wildlife watching are best at dawn or low tide.

Stay hydrated and pack snacks: Trails can be longer and more demanding than expected.

Respect park rules: Stick to designated trails and avoid disturbing wildlife or fossil sites.

What Calvert Cliffs Taught Me

Calvert Cliffs is more than a park—it's a portal to a world long gone and a reminder of nature's constant evolution. It taught me patience, curiosity, and respect for the fragile threads that connect past and present.

Have you ever felt that quiet awe when holding a relic from the distant past in your hand? Calvert Cliffs invites you to experience that wonder firsthand. And beyond the fossils, it offers peace, adventure, and a connection to the wild that lingers long after you leave.

CHAPTER 5

OUTDOOR ACTIVITIES AND ADVENTURES IN MARYLAND

HIKING AND TRAIL ADVENTURES

Maryland is a treasure trove for outdoor enthusiasts, offering a diverse array of hiking trails that cater to all levels of adventurers. From the rugged terrains of the Appalachian Trail to the tranquil paths of Patapsco Valley State Park, the state's natural beauty is both accessible and awe-inspiring.

The Appalachian Trail: A Journey Through Maryland

The Appalachian Trail (AT) meanders through Maryland for approximately 40 miles, presenting hikers with a variety of landscapes, including dense forests, rocky ridges, and panoramic vistas. Notable spots along this stretch include:

Washington Monument State Park: Home to the first monument dedicated to George Washington, this area offers a scenic overlook of the surrounding countryside.

Washington Monument State Park

Annapolis Rock: A popular destination for sunset views, providing hikers with a breathtaking panorama of the valley below.

Weverton Cliffs: Known for its challenging ascent and rewarding views, this spot is a favorite among seasoned hikers.

Camping opportunities are available near trailheads, such as the Pine Knob Shelter, allowing hikers to immerse themselves in the wilderness overnight.

Billy Goat Trail: A Test of Strength and Agility

Located within the Chesapeake and Ohio Canal National Historical Park, the Billy Goat Trail is renowned for its challenging terrain. Divided into three sections:

Section A: A strenuous 1.7-mile stretch that requires hikers to scramble over boulders and navigate steep inclines along the Potomac River's Mather Gorge.

Section B: A moderate 1.4-mile path that offers a mix of rocky and forested terrain.

Section C: An easier 1.6-mile trail suitable for families and casual hikers.

The trail provides stunning views of the Potomac River and is a must-visit for those seeking adventure and natural beauty.

Patapsco Valley State Park: A Haven for Outdoor Activities

Stretching over 14,000 acres along the Patapsco River, Patapsco Valley State Park offers a plethora of recreational activities. Highlights include:

Cascade Falls: A serene 10-foot waterfall accessible via a short hike, perfect for a refreshing dip.

Swinging Bridges: Historic suspension bridges that add a touch of adventure to your hike.

Multi-use Trails: Paths suitable for hiking, mountain biking, and horseback riding, catering to a variety of outdoor enthusiasts.

The park's diverse ecosystems and rich history make it a prime destination for nature lovers.

RV Parks Near Trailheads: Combining Adventure with Comfort

For those who prefer the comfort of RV camping, Maryland offers several parks near popular hiking trails:

Greenbrier State Park: Located in Boonsboro, this park features 164 campsites equipped with water, bathhouses, fire rings, and tables. It's pet-friendly and offers RV options.

Cunningham Falls State Park: Situated in Thurmont, this park provides campsites and mini cabins near the William Houck Area, close to hiking trails and the 78-foot Cunningham Falls.

Patapsco Valley State Park: With multiple areas offering camping facilities, this park allows visitors to stay close to nature while enjoying modern amenities.

Staying at these RV parks provides easy access to hiking trails, allowing adventurers to explore Maryland's natural beauty without sacrificing comfort.

Have you ever wondered why things seem to fall apart just when you're trying to move forward? Embarking on a challenging hike can mirror life's obstacles. The rugged terrains, unexpected twists, and moments of doubt are akin to the hurdles we face in our personal journeys. Yet, just as reaching the summit offers a sense of accomplishment and clarity, overcoming life's challenges can lead to personal growth and insight.

Tips for a Successful Hiking Adventure in Maryland:

Plan Ahead: Research trail maps, weather conditions, and park regulations before heading out.

Pack Appropriately: Bring essentials like water, snacks, a first-aid kit, and appropriate footwear.

Respect Nature: Stay on marked trails, pack out all trash, and avoid disturbing wildlife.

Know Your Limits: Choose trails that match your fitness level and experience.

Stay Informed: Check for any park alerts or reservation requirements, especially during peak seasons.

By following these guidelines, you can ensure a safe and enjoyable hiking experience in Maryland's beautiful landscapes.

Maryland's hiking trails offer a diverse range of experiences, from the challenging terrains of the Appalachian Trail and Billy Goat Trail to the serene paths of Patapsco Valley State Park. Whether you're an experienced hiker or a beginner, the state's natural beauty provides a perfect backdrop for outdoor adventures. So, lace up your boots, pack your gear, and set out to explore the trails that await you.

WATER SPORTS AND RIVER ADVENTURES

I still remember the first time I kayaked across the Chesapeake Bay. The early morning sun shimmered on the water like spilled gold, and every stroke of the paddle felt like a heartbeat. I was nervous—no, terrified—but exhilarated. Have you ever felt so small and powerful at the same time? Out there on the open water, I found something I hadn't even known I was searching for: silence, clarity, and a rush of raw freedom.

Water has always held a strange kind of magic for me. Maybe it does for you too? That draw to the unknown depths, the way rivers wind like secrets waiting to be unraveled, or how the sea stretches endlessly like a metaphor for everything you've ever hoped for.

Maryland, bordered by over 7,700 miles of shoreline, rivers, and streams, is nothing short of a playground for water lovers. Whether you're seeking the tranquil rhythm of a paddle through wetlands or the adrenaline of white-water rapids, this state delivers—and then some.

Chesapeake Bay: The Heart of Maryland's Water Life

The Chesapeake Bay is the largest estuary in the United States—and it's the beating heart of Maryland's aquatic adventures.

Kayaking and Canoeing

Glide through serene coves and winding tidal rivers. Some of the most popular kayaking areas include:

Eastern Neck National Wildlife Refuge – Spot herons, eagles, and ospreys as you paddle through untouched marshes.

Taylors Island and Blackwater National Wildlife Refuge – Known as the "Everglades of the North," this is ideal for a peaceful, almost meditative paddle.

Chesapeake Bay Environmental Center (Grasonville) – Offers rentals and guided trips through marshes and open waters.

Tip: Use lightweight kayaks and check the tides before you launch—many coves can become tricky at low tide.

Sailing and Boating

The Bay is world-renowned for sailing. Communities like Annapolis, the "Sailing Capital of America," offer:

Chartered cruises and **sailing schools**.

Regattas and competitive sailing events throughout the summer.

Calm and protected waters, ideal for beginners and seasoned sailors alike.

Ask yourself: Have you ever let the wind take control, just once, and trusted the current to carry you forward?

Fishing Havens: Reel in the Thrill

Fishing in Maryland isn't just a hobby—it's a tradition, a rite of passage, and for many, a way of life.

Chesapeake Bay Fishing

Known for **striped bass (rockfish)**, bluefish, and croaker.

Charter boats run regularly out of towns like Kent Narrows and Solomons.

Shore fishing spots abound—look for piers in Sandy Point State Park or Matapeake.

Potomac River

Best for **smallmouth bass**, **catfish**, and even **snakehead** fishing.

Great access from **Great Falls**, **Seneca Creek**, and **Point of Rocks**.

Kayak fishing is especially popular near Brunswick and the Monocacy River confluence.

Susquehanna River

Flowing from Pennsylvania into the Upper Chesapeake, the Susquehanna offers:

Prime fishing for **walleye**, **perch**, and **largemouth bass**.

Great shore access at **Port Deposit** and **Havre de Grace**.

Fishing tip: Check seasonal regulations and licensing requirements—rules change for tidal vs. non-tidal waters.

River Rafting and Whitewater Thrills

Yes, Maryland has whitewater. You just have to know where to look.

Upper Potomac River (Western Maryland)

Harpers Ferry to Brunswick offers Class I–III rapids—perfect for beginners and families.

Guided rafting companies operate seasonally and provide all gear and safety training.

Youghiogheny River (Western Edge)

While mostly in Pennsylvania, the Youghiogheny dips into Maryland and offers thrilling **Class IV rapids**.

Adventure Sports Center International (ASCI) in McHenry simulates rapids for training or recreational use—perfect for practicing before tackling real rivers.

Have you ever faced a rapid in your life—not the kind made of water, but the emotional kind? When you're tossed from side to side, unsure if you'll make it to the calm? That's what whitewater teaches you: balance, trust, resilience.

RV Campgrounds with Waterfront Access

Camping doesn't have to mean sacrificing luxury. Maryland has some stellar **RV-friendly campgrounds** with **direct water access**, ideal for blending relaxation with adventure.

Assateague Island National Seashore

Oceanfront RV camping.

Paddleboarding, surf fishing, and kayaking in Sinepuxent Bay.

Bonus: Wild ponies roam the island. Yes, wild ponies.

Elk Neck State Park

Located on a peninsula between the Elk River and Chesapeake Bay.

Boat ramps, a sandy beach, and kayak rentals.

Nearby trails lead to the iconic **Turkey Point Lighthouse**.

Point Lookout State Park

Located at the southern tip of Maryland.

Surrounded by water on three sides—Potomac River meets the Chesapeake.

Ideal for kayaking, crabbing, and surf fishing.

Greenbrier State Park

Has a man-made lake with a swimming beach and kayak rentals.

RV hookups and wooded sites for privacy.

If you've ever dreamed of waking up to the sound of water lapping at the shore, of sipping your morning coffee while watching the fog lift off the river, these parks offer that dream on repeat.

Essential Gear and Safety Tips

Always wear a PFD (personal flotation device) – Non-negotiable.

Check weather and tide charts before heading out—conditions can change fast.

Invest in dry bags to keep your gear safe.

Bring sun protection – sunscreen, sunglasses with straps, and a hat.

Know the water access rules – Some parks require permits or reservations.

Maryland's waterways don't just offer recreation—they offer reflection. Whether you're drifting down the Susquehanna at sunrise, casting your line into the Potomac, or testing your courage in the whitewater, each experience writes a story into your memory.

And here's the best part: You don't need to be a professional athlete, or a sailor, or even all that brave. You just need a willingness to step in, to get a little wet, and to let Maryland's rivers, bays, and lakes show you something new about the world—and yourself.

So, what's holding you back? Is it fear? Uncertainty? Or is it just the comfort of routine? Maybe it's time to trade routine for river, and fear for freedom. The water's waiting.

FISHING AND WILDLIFE WATCHING IN MARYLAND

I can still feel the early morning dew soaking through my shoes as I stepped onto the soft earth of the Eastern Shore. The world was hushed, except for the distant call of a blue heron and the gentle lapping of water against the reeds. I wasn't there to catch anything extraordinary—just to sit, to be still, and maybe cast a line. But that morning, something extraordinary happened anyway. A bald eagle soared overhead. Not in a zoo. Not on a screen. Right there, above me—wild and free.

Have you ever experienced a moment that was so pure, so perfect, that it forced you to stop and just be? That's what nature in Maryland does. It reaches inside you and stirs something ancient, something essential.

Maryland isn't just diverse in its landscapes—it's alive. Teeming with migratory birds, freshwater and saltwater fish, and wildlife that thrive in marshes, forests, rivers, and coastline, the state is a paradise for outdoor explorers. Whether you're an angler, birder, or simply someone who finds peace in a pair of binoculars and a quiet path, this state delivers.

Top Spots for Wildlife Watching

Blackwater National Wildlife Refuge in Cambridge is often called the "Everglades of the North" and is the premier birding destination in the state. You can spot bald eagles, great blue herons, snowy egrets, red-winged blackbirds, and migratory waterfowl. Fall and winter are best for bird migrations, and spring is excellent for nesting behavior. The refuge offers wildlife driving tours, photography opportunities, kayaking in the marshes, and hiking on flat trails like the Marsh Edge Trail. A spotting scope is recommended for close views without disturbing the wildlife.

Eastern Neck National Wildlife Refuge in Rock Hall is another birding gem, home to over 250 species of birds, including tundra swans, ospreys, and warblers. The island features walking trails and observation decks and is especially rewarding during fall migrations.

Catoctin Mountain Park and Cunningham Falls State Park are great for spotting deer, foxes, woodpeckers, and occasionally black bears. These parks combine wildlife watching with waterfall hikes and scenic ridge-top views.

Fishing in Maryland: Saltwater, Freshwater & Everything In Between

Fishing in Maryland isn't just a pastime—it's embedded in the culture.

Saltwater fishing is best along the Chesapeake Bay and Atlantic Ocean. Popular catches include striped bass (rockfish), bluefish, croaker, flounder, and blue crabs. Charter services are widely available in Solomons, Kent Island, and Ocean City. The Susquehanna Flats are especially known in spring for trophy-size striped bass.

Freshwater fishing is available across over 100 lakes and countless rivers. Deep Creek Lake in Western Maryland is a hotspot for smallmouth bass, trout, and walleye. Gunpowder Falls and the Savage River are fly fishing havens, stocked with brown and rainbow trout. The Potomac River offers excellent largemouth bass and catfish fishing, especially near Brunswick and Great Falls.

Fishing access varies by location, so it's important to check the Maryland Department of Natural Resources for licenses and regulations, especially for tidal versus non-tidal waters. Many public parks have piers, cleaning stations, and ADA-accessible fishing spots.

RV Campgrounds for Outdoor Lovers

Tuckahoe State Park is located near the Eastern Shore's birding and fishing hot spots, with opportunities for boating and canoeing on Tuckahoe Lake and shaded, wooded RV sites.

Cherry Hill RV Park in College Park provides more urban amenities while still offering access to Greenbelt Park and Patuxent Research Refuge for birdwatching.

Pocomoke River State Park sits along a hauntingly beautiful, tannin rich river and offers boat rentals, nature programs, and proximity to Assateague Island, known for its wild horses.

Deep Creek Lake State Park offers boat docks, fishing for walleye, and forest trails filled with owl calls and porcupine sightings.

Essential Wildlife Watching Tips

Go early or late—dawn and dusk are prime times for most wildlife activity. Be quiet and patient. Bring binoculars or a camera with a zoom lens to observe wildlife from a respectful distance. Wear natural colors to blend in. Check seasonal migrations, as Maryland's bird populations change dramatically throughout the year.

Essential Fishing Tips for Maryland

Check the tide charts for coastal fishing. Bring bug spray, especially in summer. Match your gear to your target species. Learn local fishing etiquette—many Maryland anglers are generous with tips if approached respectfully.

Reflect and Reconnect

Have you ever wondered what it would feel like to really connect again? Not through screens, but through stillness? Maryland's forests, rivers, and marshes don't just offer nature—they offer a return to yourself. To something older, quieter, more honest. Fishing isn't just about the fish. Watching wildlife isn't just about ticking species off a list. It's about paying attention. Learning to be still. To listen.

Whether you're pulling in a trophy bass or watching a bald eagle take flight, these moments matter. They remind us that we are not separate from the wild—we're a part of it. And in Maryland, that wild is just a short drive away.

CHAPTER 6

EXPLORING MARYLAND'S ICONIC CITIES

BALTIMORE: CULTURE, HISTORY, AND HARBOR

A City That Stole My Breath—And Then Gave It Back

I still remember the first time I laid eyes on Baltimore's Inner Harbor. It wasn't just the skyline or the shimmering water under the soft light of a spring morning. It was something deeper—a hum in the air, a sense of history whispering through the cobbled streets, the warm laughter of street musicians, and the unexpected sense that I had stepped into a living, breathing canvas of culture and memory.

I was on a cross-country RV trip at the time, chasing something I couldn't quite name. Restlessness? Purpose? Healing? Maybe all three. I arrived in Baltimore weary but curious. Little did I know this city—so often misrepresented, so deeply layered—would become one of the most surprising and transformative chapters of my journey.

Have you ever walked into a place and felt like it had been waiting for you? Like it held answers you didn't know you were looking for?

That was Baltimore for me.

Inner Harbor: Where Stories Begin

The Inner Harbor is not just a tourist attraction—it's the soul of Baltimore. As I strolled along the waterfront promenade, the view of historic ships docked alongside modern museums felt like an invitation to step between centuries.

The USS Constellation, floating silently in the harbor, pulled me in with its haunting beauty. Climbing aboard, I could almost hear the footsteps of sailors past, feel the creak of timber beneath their boots, and sense the pulse of history running through the ship's spine.

Close by, the **National Aquarium** held another kind of wonder—otherworldly colors and creatures that reminded me how much mystery still exists below the surface of things. I spent hours here, mesmerized not just by jellyfish and sharks, but by the sheer intricacy of ecosystems that mirror our own lives—complex, fragile, interdependent.

And that's the thing about Baltimore: it invites you to see connections. Between past and present. Between chaos and calm. Between yourself and the stories that shaped this place.

Museums That Spark Wonder and Wisdom

I'm a museum junkie. Always have been. But Baltimore's offerings struck a different chord. These weren't just buildings filled with artifacts—they were active, immersive experiences that shook loose memories and inspired new thinking.

The **Maryland Science Center** rekindled the child in me. I laughed out loud during a planetarium show, eyes wide as galaxies spun overhead. It was a reminder that awe is an emotion adults should chase more often. When was the last time you let yourself be amazed by something bigger than you?

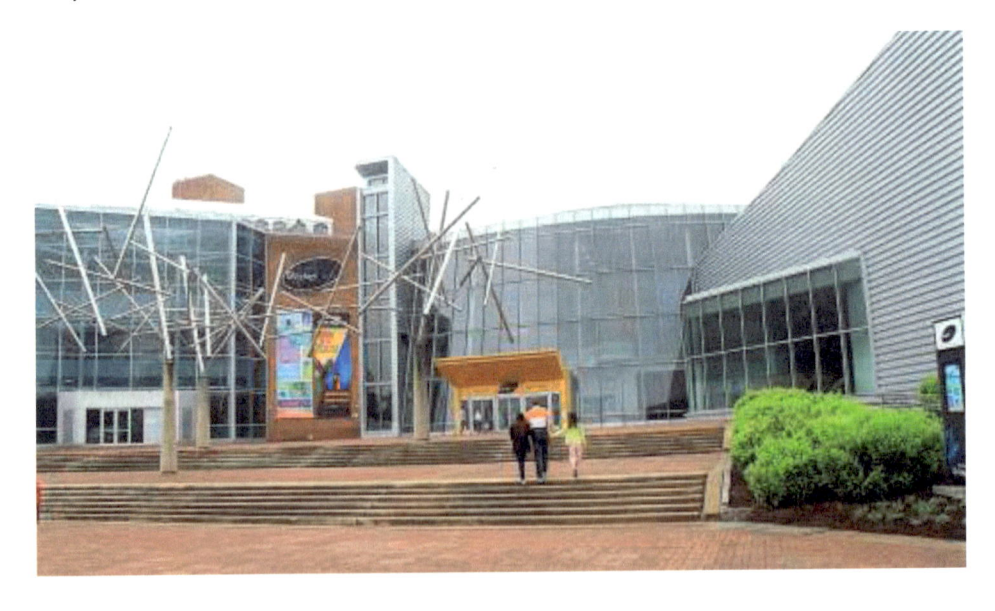

Maryland Science Center

Then there was the **Walters Art Museum**, tucked away like a well-kept secret. Inside, centuries of global art whispered stories of empires and everyday life, love and war, faith and defiance. One particular exhibit—a Roman-era sculpture with a broken nose and eroded smile—stopped me cold. There was a strange comfort in its imperfection. It made me ask: Why do we hide our cracks when they're the very things that prove we've lived?

Where to Park and Stay: RV-Friendly Baltimore

Finding an RV park near a major city is often like trying to squeeze an elephant through a keyhole. But Baltimore surprised me again—there are several spots that make urban exploration both easy and comfortable.

Top RV Parks Near Baltimore:

Cherry Hill Park (College Park, MD)

Approx. 30-40 minutes from downtown Baltimore

Full amenities, public transit access, clean facilities

Pro Tip: Use the Metro to avoid city traffic—it's stress-free and scenic.

Bar Harbor RV Park & Marina (Abingdon, MD)

Waterfront views, about 25 minutes from the Inner Harbor

Quiet, peaceful, and stunning sunset vistas

I watched a heron land on the dock one evening—pure magic.

Patapsco Valley State Park (Elkridge, MD)

For those who crave a mix of nature and city

Hiking trails, forested serenity, and quick access to Baltimore

Ideal for resetting your energy before diving back into city life.

Planning is essential—especially if you're traveling during peak seasons. I learned the hard way: one night of last minute hunting led me to a Walmart parking lot and a restless, noisy sleep. Book early. Trust me.

The Pulse of the City: Neighborhoods, Food, and Local Charm

Once you've soaked in the harbor and museums, it's time to get local. Baltimore is a city of neighborhoods, each with its own heartbeat.

Fells Point: Cobblestone streets, pubs older than most buildings in the country, and the kind of seafood that makes you want to write poetry. I devoured a crab cake here that changed my life. No exaggeration.

Mount Vernon: The cultural center, home to the original Washington Monument (sorry, D.C.), and the Peabody Library—a space so beautiful it will steal your breath.

Hampden: Quirky, colorful, and unapologetically weird. Think vintage shops, murals, and locals who'll tell you stories if you just ask. Have you ever connected with a stranger who made your day better? You will here.

What Baltimore Taught Me

Baltimore taught me that beauty and grit can—and should—coexist. That cities are like people: layered, flawed, evolving. That sometimes, the places we expect the least from are the ones that give us the most.

It also reminded me of the importance of staying open. To new places, new stories, new emotions. That travel isn't about escape. It's about presence.

So I ask you—**what are you really searching for on your journey?**

Is it rest? Discovery? Forgiveness? Fun?

Whatever it is, Baltimore just might have a piece of the answer.

Quick Travel Tips for Visiting Baltimore in an RV

Avoid rush hour when driving in or out—especially on I-95 and I-83.

Use public transit or bike rentals within the city—it's easier than parking.

Always double-check height clearances when driving downtown. Some streets and garages are RV nightmares.

Pack for all weather—Baltimore can flip from sunny to stormy fast, especially near the water.

Talk to locals—they'll steer you to the best crab spots, the hidden murals, the live jazz cafes you'll remember forever.

ANNAPOLIS: MARYLAND'S STATE CAPITAL

A City Anchored in History, Drifting in Charm

The morning I arrived in Annapolis was shrouded in soft fog, the kind that makes everything feel quieter, slower, sacred. I parked my RV just outside the city, brewed a quick cup of coffee, and sat in silence as the mist gave way to sunlight. Before I even walked a single cobbled street, I felt it: Annapolis wasn't just a stop—it was a pause. A place where time loosened its grip and history leaned in close.

Have you ever visited somewhere that made you feel like you were walking through the pages of a storybook? Not a fantasy—but a rich, textured chronicle of lives lived with pride, purpose, and tradition?

That's Annapolis.

The U.S. Naval Academy: Discipline and Legacy on Display

There's a reverent stillness that settles over you as you step onto the grounds of the **U.S. Naval Academy**. You can feel it in the way cadets carry themselves, in the sharp lines of their uniforms, in the thunderous silence of the **Naval Academy Chapel**, where midshipmen come to reflect.

I took a guided tour, led by a retired officer who wove tales of courage, heartbreak, and tradition into every corner we explored. Inside **Bancroft Hall**—the largest college dormitory in the world—I saw not just living quarters, but the heartbeat of an institution that molds boys and girls into guardians of the sea.

Standing in **Memorial Hall**, I stared up at a flag flown at Iwo Jima and felt a wave of emotion I hadn't expected. Pride. Grief. Gratitude. It hit me that these weren't just students. They were stories waiting to unfold—many of them on the front lines of history.

Ask yourself this: When was the last time you stood somewhere that demanded your respect? That reminded you of the weight of sacrifice?

Colonial Streets, Waterfront Beats

From the Naval Academy, I wandered into the **Historic District**, where brick sidewalks cradled the soles of my boots and gas lamps cast golden glows even in daylight. I was struck by how *alive* everything felt—despite the centuries behind it.

Every building whispered: "We've stood the test of time."

State Circle, home to the **Maryland State House**—the oldest U.S. state capitol in continuous legislative use—offered a history lesson you could walk through. Inside, I stood in the chamber where George Washington resigned his commission as commander-in-chief of the Continental Army. The same walls. The same floorboards. It made the Revolutionary War feel like it happened yesterday.

And yet, Annapolis never feels like a city stuck in the past. Walk a few blocks, and you'll be sipping craft cocktails in a sleek bar, or watching paddleboarders glide across **Spa Creek** like it's the most natural thing in the world.

Dining by the Water: A Feast for the Senses

Let's talk about food—and not just food, but *experiences* around food.

One evening, I found myself at **Chart House**, seated outside with the sun bleeding gold into the harbor. Boats bobbed gently as waiters danced between tables. I ordered the crab-stuffed shrimp and a glass of chilled Sauvignon Blanc. Each bite felt like a love letter to the Chesapeake Bay.

But it wasn't just the fine dining that stood out. It was the smaller moments. Like grabbing a bagel at **Bakers & Co.** in Eastport and watching locals sip espresso like it was a morning ritual passed down through generations. Or devouring oysters at **Osteria 177** while eavesdropping on an older couple debating the best sailing routes in the bay.

Food in Annapolis doesn't just feed you. It roots you.

RV-Friendly Campgrounds Near Annapolis

If you're traveling by RV, you'll be thrilled to know that Annapolis offers several comfortable and convenient basecamps that keep you close to the charm while giving you space to breathe.

1. **Capitol KOA (Millersville, MD)**

Only 20 minutes from downtown Annapolis

Full hook-ups, clean restrooms, pool, and Wi-Fi

Shaded, peaceful, and perfect for extended stays

Bonus: Frequent shuttles into the city during peak seasons

2. **Bayshore Campground (Rock Hall, MD)**

A bit farther, but worth it for waterfront views of the Chesapeake

Ideal if you want a beachy vibe while staying close to the capital

Great for kayaking, fishing, and long, reflective walks along the bay

3. **Patuxent River Park (Jug Bay Natural Area)**

Rustic, tranquil, and nature-forward

About 40 minutes from Annapolis

Best for those who enjoy quiet camping with hiking trails and birdwatching

I stayed at Capitol KOA, and it struck the perfect balance—convenient access to the city and a quiet retreat at the end of each packed day.

Maritime Soul: Sailing, Sunsets, and Serenity

Annapolis is often called the *Sailing Capital of the U.S.*, and it earns the title every time the wind shifts and sails unfurl across the bay. Even if you've never set foot on a boat, the allure is magnetic.

One afternoon, I booked a sunset cruise aboard the historic **Schooner Woodwind**. As we sliced through the waves, sails snapping above, I felt something I hadn't in a long time: light. Free. Unburdened.

There's something spiritual about being on the water here. It's not just leisure— it's heritage. Every breeze carries the echo of generations of sailors, dreamers, and wanderers.

Have you ever felt completely in tune with the elements—wind, water, sun—and forgotten for a moment that you were just passing through?

Annapolis Isn't Just a Place—It's a Feeling

Annapolis Map

It's the sound of church bells echoing through colonial streets.

The splash of oars on quiet waters at dawn.

The rustle of flags against masts in a harbor that never sleeps.

Annapolis reminds you that history isn't something dusty and removed—it's alive, beating in every corner of this vibrant, compact city. Whether you're in search of meaning, beauty, relaxation, or inspiration, Annapolis offers it not with grand fanfare, but with subtle, enduring grace.

Travel Tips for RVers Exploring Annapolis:

Reserve early, especially in spring and fall—peak sailing and festival seasons.

Use the Annapolis Circulator Bus to navigate the city without worrying about parking.

Bring walking shoes—Annapolis is best explored on foot.

Look for local events like the U.S. Sailboat Show or Colonial Candlelight Tours.

Respect the pace—this isn't a city to rush through. Let it unfold at its own rhythm.

OCEAN CITY: A BEACH LOVER'S PARADISE

Where Salt Air Heals, and Memories Live Forever

When I first rolled into Ocean City, Maryland, my windows were down, music was loud, and I could already smell the salt in the air long before I saw the beach. There's something about beach towns, isn't there? That mix of nostalgia, sun-fueled freedom, and gentle chaos that feels like summer has decided to stay forever.

I wasn't planning to fall in love with Ocean City. I was chasing warm weather and open skies. But this place—this coastal ribbon of laughter, sunscreen, and motion—grabbed my heart before I had a chance to think twice.

Have you ever arrived somewhere and realized, almost instantly, that you needed exactly what it had to offer?

That was Ocean City for me. And it might be for you, too.

The Boardwalk: America's Playground by the Sea

There's no way to talk about Ocean City without starting with its legendary **boardwalk**. Stretching over three miles, it's a living, breathing carnival of sights, sounds, and tastes.

By day, the sun bathes the wooden planks in gold as families weave between **Thrasher's French Fries**, **Dolle's saltwater taffy**, and shops selling everything from airbrushed T-shirts to handmade jewelry. I grabbed a fresh-squeezed lemonade and just walked. No plan. Just letting the tide of people and energy pull me along.

At night, the scene shifts. Street performers light up the dusk with fire juggling, music, and laughter. Neon flickers from arcades and pizza joints. The **Ocean City Pier** bursts into life, with its rickety rides and dizzying nostalgia. I rode the Ferris wheel alone and stared out at the Atlantic in silence. Sometimes, healing comes not in stillness, but in motion.

Question for you: When was the last time you let go and let a place carry you?

Beach Days and Salt-Kissed Skin

If you came to Ocean City for the beach, you're in the right place.

Every morning, I'd make coffee in the RV, grab a towel, and hit the sand. You don't need a plan. The ocean sets the schedule here.

I spent lazy afternoons under an umbrella with a book I never quite finished. I watched kids build sandcastles that would soon be washed away—beautiful reminders of impermanence. I waded waist-deep into the surf and let the waves knock the anxiety right out of me.

Whether you're chasing sunrise jogs, afternoon volleyball, or evening bonfires, this beach doesn't disappoint. It holds you, like a mother who knows you've had a long journey.

Fishing, Boating, and Water Adventures

For those of us who find therapy in fishing lines and drifting boats, Ocean City is paradise.

I booked a charter trip one morning—just me, a few strangers, and a captain who'd been doing this since he could walk. As we headed out into deeper water, I felt the land fall away behind me, and with it, a few burdens I didn't know I was still carrying.

I caught my first flounder that day. Not a big one. But it was mine. And the moment felt bigger than it looked.

You don't have to go offshore to enjoy Ocean City's water adventures. Rent a **jet ski**, take a **sunset paddleboard ride in Assawoman Bay**, or book a spot on a **family-friendly pirate cruise** (yes, it's as cheesy and fun as it sounds).

Nightlife: Ocean City After Dark

If the beach is for recharging, the nights are for reawakening.

Ocean City's nightlife is surprisingly diverse. Want laid-back drinks with live acoustic music? Check out **Seacrets**, a sprawling waterfront bar where you can sip cocktails with your feet in the bay. Looking for something louder? Try **Fager's**

Island, where the sunset celebration feels almost sacred, followed by DJ sets that keep you dancing.

And for those who want to keep it family-friendly? Grab a soft-serve cone from **King Kone** and take an evening walk under the string lights. The laughter of strangers and the hum of the Atlantic will keep you company.

Best RV Parks Near the Ocean

Here's where things get practical. Ocean City is RV-friendly—**if you plan ahead.** The beach draws huge crowds in summer, so booking your campground in advance is non-negotiable.

1. **Frontier Town RV Resort & Campground**

Located in Berlin, just 5 miles from Ocean City

Western-themed resort with a water park, lazy river, and private beach access

Shuttle service to Ocean City

Best for families or travelers looking for *fun with amenities*

2. **Castaways RV Resort & Campground**

Waterfront property with both standard and luxury RV sites

Tiki bar, dog beach, kayak rentals, and live weekend music

Waking up here feels like being on your own private island

3. **Sun Outdoors Ocean City Gateway**

More low-key and quiet, located slightly inland

Still close to the action but with a peaceful, family-friendly vibe

Great for longer stays and those who prefer a blend of city and countryside

The Hidden Side of Ocean City

If you look past the neon and noise, Ocean City has another layer. One morning I woke up before sunrise and walked the beach alone. No music. No crowd. Just me and the Atlantic.

The sky turned from navy to lavender, then burst into a flaming orange crescendo. For a few minutes, the world stood still. And in that moment, I realized something: joy doesn't always come crashing in with fanfare. Sometimes, it arrives quietly, gently, like the first rays of morning light.

Tips for RVers Exploring Ocean City

Book early, especially from Memorial Day to Labor Day.

Use park-and-ride lots or local buses to get into town—driving and parking an RV near the boardwalk can be a nightmare.

Pack bug spray—marshy areas can be mosquito-heavy at dusk.

Bring bikes or rent locally—perfect for cruising the boardwalk early in the morning.

Stay flexible—weather shifts fast by the sea, and that spontaneous rain shower might be the most refreshing moment of your day.

Ocean City Isn't Just a Vacation Spot—It's a State of Mind

It's where time slows and smiles come easy.

Where the waves don't just crash—they cleanse.

Where you can be a kid again, no matter how many miles you've driven or years you've carried.

Ocean City reminded me that joy doesn't have to be chased. Sometimes, it's waiting for you on a beach towel, with sand in your hair and the sound of seagulls overhead.

So I ask you—**what kind of happiness are you searching for?**

Because chances are, you'll find a piece of it here.

CHAPTER 7

HISTORY, CULTURE, AND HERITAGE IN MARYLAND

THE CIVIL WAR'S ROLE IN MARYLAND'S HISTORY

Where Conflict Carved a State's Soul and Echoes Still Whisper Through the Land

I'll never forget the first time I stood on the blood-soaked fields of **Antietam**.

The morning was eerily still. Fog hung low, clinging to the golden grasses like ghosts reluctant to leave. As I walked the gentle slopes near Burnside's Bridge, I could feel something in the air—a weight, a sorrow, an energy that had survived centuries. This wasn't just history. It was grief frozen in time.

I'd read about the Civil War, sure. I'd studied the maps, memorized the names—Lee, McClellan, Lincoln. But nothing prepares you for standing where over 22,000 men fell in a single day. It hits differently when the past has a heartbeat.

Have you ever found yourself in a place where time stands still? Where your breath shortens and your skin prickles because you *feel* the past pressing in from every angle?

That's what Maryland gave me. And if you let it, it will give that to you too.

Maryland: A Border State with a Fractured Heart

It's easy to forget just how precarious Maryland's position was during the Civil War. A **border state**—not fully North, not fully South—its loyalties were split like the nation itself.

Families here were torn apart, neighbors became enemies, and entire towns lived in daily fear of being burned or broken by advancing armies. The **Mason-Dixon Line** may have been a geographic divider, but Maryland was the emotional fault line—shaking, cracking, aching under the strain of a war that demanded allegiance at all costs.

President Lincoln even took the unprecedented step of suspending **habeas corpus** in Maryland to prevent secession. Can you imagine living in a state where civil liberties are paused and military authority reigns, all to keep your home from slipping into chaos?

Understanding Maryland's Civil War history isn't just about battles—it's about identity, resistance, survival.

Antietam National Battlefield: A Day That Changed Everything

September 17, 1862. The single bloodiest day in American military history.

That's the kind of fact you read and nod at—until you stand on the fields of **Antietam** and imagine 12 hours of relentless gunfire, screaming, smoke, and dying hope.

I walked the Sunken Road—also known as **Bloody Lane**—in silence. And I cried. Not because I was sad, but because I felt the *truth* of it. Young men, many barely old enough to shave, gave everything on that ground. For country, for ideology, for orders they may not have even fully understood.

The National Park Service does an excellent job preserving the battlefield, and the interpretive center provides context that is deeply moving. But nothing replaces walking those fields for yourself.

Take a guided tour. Even better—talk to a reenactor or park ranger. They carry the stories in their bones.

Harpers Ferry National Historical Park: Where the Spark Caught Fire

Technically located in West Virginia, **Harpers Ferry** is a short drive from Maryland and an essential piece of the puzzle.

This is where **John Brown**, the radical abolitionist, staged his doomed raid in 1859, hoping to ignite a nationwide slave uprising. His plan failed—but the impact did not. His trial, execution, and the fear he stirred in the South helped push the nation to the brink of war.

The town of Harpers Ferry is stunning, nestled at the confluence of the Potomac and Shenandoah Rivers. Walking through the preserved buildings, you can see the cracks of history everywhere—bullet holes, charred wood, weathered signs.

I sat on a bench overlooking the river and wondered: What does it take to risk everything for a cause? Do we even know anymore what we're willing to sacrifice for what we believe in?

Fort McHenry: The Star-Spangled Survivor

Fort McHenry

Everyone knows the anthem. Few know the place.

Fort McHenry, located right in Baltimore, is where Francis Scott Key penned the words to *The Star-Spangled Banner* after watching British forces bomb the fort during the War of 1812. But the fort also played a significant role during the Civil War.

Used as a military prison, it housed political dissenters and Confederate sympathizers under Lincoln's emergency war measures. In many ways, it symbolizes the complex intersection of patriotism and civil rights—a theme that feels just as relevant today.

Walk the ramparts. Watch the flag ripple in the wind. You'll never hear the anthem the same way again.

RV Parks and Civil War Camping Near the Conflict

Whether you're a history buff, a curious traveler, or someone searching for personal meaning through national memory, staying near these historic sites makes the experience immersive.

1. **Greenbrier State Park (Near Antietam)**

RV-friendly with electric hookups

Wooded serenity and a lake for swimming or kayaking

Just a short drive to Antietam Battlefield

2. **Harpers Ferry Campground**

Stunning river views and close access to the town

Perfect for combining nature with history

Can get crowded in peak season—book early!

3. **Cherry Hill Park (Near Fort McHenry & D.C.)**

Full-service RV resort with easy access to Baltimore

Shuttle options to city attractions

Amenities galore, ideal for families or longer stays

4. **Yogi Bear's Jellystone Park (Hagerstown, MD)**

Family-focused, clean, and loaded with activities

A short drive to both Antietam and South Mountain battlefields

Great for combining fun with educational travel

How the Past Can Shape Your Present

Spending time in Maryland's Civil War landscapes did more than educate me. It *changed* me.

It made me think about my own battles. The divides in my life. The relationships that fractured when I stood at a personal crossroads. It reminded me that wounds take time to heal—sometimes generations—and that conflict, while painful, can be transformative.

So I ask you:

Are there parts of your past that feel like battlefields?

Places you return to in your mind, where something was lost—or maybe, something was born?

Visiting these sites isn't just a history lesson. It's a mirror.

Tips for Exploring Maryland's Civil War Heritage by RV

Bring a good pair of walking shoes. Many battlefields stretch across miles of open land.

Download historical audio guides. They make your self-guided experience richer.

Visit during off-peak times. Spring and fall offer cooler weather and fewer crowds.

Pack for sudden weather changes. Maryland can be unpredictable, especially in the mountains and near the water.

Talk to park rangers. Their passion is infectious, and their stories will linger longer than any plaque or signpost.

The Battle Beneath the Surface

Maryland's Civil War history isn't just etched into stone and soil—it's etched into the heart of America. Here, you don't just *learn* history. You *feel* it. You walk it. You carry it with you.

In the quiet of Antietam, the defiance of Harpers Ferry, the patriotism of Fort McHenry—you find fragments of your own story, reflected in a nation still striving to become whole.

So, will you stand where soldiers once stood?

Will you listen to the past—not just to remember, but to understand?

Maryland is waiting.

THE LEGACY OF THE CHESAPEAKE BAY

Where Water Holds Memory, and Culture Runs as Deep as the Tides

The first time I stood on the shores of the **Chesapeake Bay**, the water was perfectly still. It mirrored the sky so completely that for a moment, I felt like I was staring at the edge of the world.

I wasn't prepared for the silence—not the absence of sound, but the kind of silence that speaks. That hums with the energy of generations who've lived and died by this bay, who've hauled nets heavy with rockfish, who've patched sails in salt-stained harbors, who've watched the tides not just for leisure, but for survival.

Have you ever been somewhere that didn't just show you beauty, but whispered, *"This is where it all begins"*?

That's the Chesapeake.

A Bay That Breathes Life Into a Region

Stretching across **64,000 square miles**, the Chesapeake Bay is more than just the largest estuary in the United States—it's the *lifeblood* of Maryland. It touches nearly every facet of the state's identity, from economy to ecology, from cuisine to culture.

This isn't just a body of water. It's a *legacy*—one that has fed families, inspired artists, shaped industries, and defined communities for centuries.

The **fishing culture**, in particular, is sacred. Watermen—those rugged, salt-of-the-earth souls who head out before sunrise—aren't just catching crabs or oysters. They're carrying forward a tradition that's older than the nation itself.

I spent one morning with a local waterman in **Solomons**, watching him haul crab pots with fingers tough as barnacles. He didn't talk much. He didn't need to. His hands told the story. Callused. Precise. Reverent. This was more than a job. It was a pact—with nature, with history, with identity.

Crabs, Oysters, and Culture: The Bay on a Plate

Let's be honest: Maryland's obsession with **blue crabs** isn't just about taste—it's about *tradition*. A crab feast isn't a meal. It's a ritual.

I joined a family one weekend at a roadside seafood shack near **St. Michaels**. We sat at a picnic table covered in brown paper, wooden mallets in hand, crab shells flying like confetti. Old Bay seasoning hung thick in the air, and laughter came easy.

That night, I realized: This is what the Bay gives us—**connection**. To land, to water, to each other.

But it's not all celebration. The **oyster population**, once the pride of the Bay, has plummeted due to overharvesting and pollution. Restoration efforts are underway, but it's a sobering reminder that **our choices shape the future of these waters**.

Have you ever loved a place so much it made you want to protect it? That's what the Chesapeake does. It doesn't just give—it teaches responsibility.

Museums That Tell the Bay's Story

If you want to *understand* the Chesapeake—not just see it—you need to visit the places where its story is preserved, interpreted, and brought to life.

1. **Calvert Marine Museum (Solomons, MD)**

Stepping into this museum is like walking into a living time capsule. You'll find **prehistoric fossils**, detailed exhibits on **Chesapeake ecology**, and even a working **lighthouse**. But the heart of the museum is its watermen's heritage wing. Listening to oral histories of the bay's earliest fishing families—it moved me in ways I didn't expect.

2. **Chesapeake Bay Maritime Museum (St. Michaels, MD)**

This isn't just a museum—it's a *working campus*. You can watch historic boats being restored by hand, see a waterman's shanty, and even climb aboard a skipjack. I lost hours here, wandering the docks, listening to gulls, and watching wood shavings fall like snow in the boatyard.

If you've ever wanted to touch history—not through glass, but with your own two hands—this is the place to do it.

RV Campgrounds Near the Bay: Wake Up to Water, Wind, and Wonder

There's something magical about parking your RV near the Bay, waking up to soft lapping waves and the cry of ospreys.

1. **Tuckahoe State Park (Queen Anne, MD)**

Tuckahoe State Park

Nestled between farmland and forest, this park offers electric sites and trails that wind toward quiet tributaries.

Great base for exploring Easton, St. Michaels, and other Bay-side towns.

2. **Point Lookout State Park (Scotland, MD)**

Located where the Potomac meets the Chesapeake—jaw-dropping water views.

Historic Civil War POW site, eerie and humbling.

Fantastic fishing pier and access to calm bay kayaking.

3. **Elk Neck State Park (North East, MD)**

Scenic bluffs overlooking the Upper Bay.

Gorgeous sunsets and a rugged lighthouse trail.

Ideal for nature lovers who also want access to towns like Havre de Grace.

Environmental Stewardship: A Bay at a Crossroads

But let's not romanticize it too much—**the Chesapeake Bay is in trouble.** Nitrogen runoff, plastic pollution, climate change—it's all here, eating away at this fragile ecosystem.

Still, there's hope.

I met volunteers with the **Chesapeake Bay Foundation** planting oyster beds, cleaning shorelines, and educating visitors. Their work is proof that love for this place runs deep.

What are you doing to protect the places you love?

That's the question the Bay asks of everyone who visits. It doesn't scold—it invites. It says, *"Help me thrive, and I'll give you everything."*

The Chesapeake Is a Living Soul

To stand by this water is to stand in the flow of **time, memory, and meaning**.

You feel it in your bones—the way the tide returns without fail, the way the light dances on the surface like it's telling a secret. You feel the resilience, the pain, the pride. And if you listen closely enough, you just might hear the whispers of watermen, sailors, and stewards who've called this bay home for centuries.

So I'll ask you this:

Where does your legacy live?

Is it in a place? A memory? A ritual as simple as cracking a crab shell on a summer afternoon?

For Maryland, that legacy flows through the Chesapeake Bay.

And it's calling you.

NATIVE AMERICAN AND AFRICAN AMERICAN HERITAGE

Voices That Shaped the Land, Stories That Refuse to Be Forgotten

I remember standing in Piscataway Park, facing the wide Potomac River, with the wind brushing through the reeds. The sky was overcast, a kind of silvery grey that seemed to make everything more alive. As I looked across the water toward Mount Vernon, it hit me—I was standing on sacred land. Land that had carried the feet, the stories, the lives of indigenous peoples for thousands of years before "Maryland" ever had a name.

It's easy to see monuments and museums and think history lives in the past. But in Maryland, you realize—history is alive. It pulses through the soil, it lingers in the air, and most powerfully, it speaks through the stories of those who endured, resisted, and built legacies under impossible conditions.

Have you ever walked through a place and felt like the ground itself was trying to tell you something?

Because if you open your heart and your ears in Maryland, you will hear it: the echo of Native drums, the hum of spirituals sung in resistance, the whispers of ancestors who survived despite everything.

Indigenous Maryland: The Land Before the Colony

Long before colonial ships arrived, Native American tribes lived in what we now call Maryland—Piscataway, Nanticoke, Susquehannock, and others. They fished these waters, hunted these forests, and honored this land with rituals and reverence we can still learn from today.

When I visited Piscataway Park, I felt a reverence I hadn't expected. This isn't a place of flashy signage or loud storytelling—it's quiet, humble, and sacred. Here, the Piscataway people, who were one of the largest tribal nations in the region, still maintain a presence. The accidental beauty of the place—its stillness, its wildlife, the soft whisper of wind through marsh grass—makes it perfect for quiet reflection.

You can visit the National Colonial Farm on the site to get a sense of colonial life, but don't miss the interpretive events and storytelling programs led by Native leaders. They give voice to the generations erased from textbooks.

Tip: Check for seasonal festivals and heritage events—many involve drumming, dancing, and oral storytelling, creating a vivid window into the indigenous spirit of the region.

African American Roots: From Slavery to Self-Determination

To understand Maryland, you must understand the Black experience here.

This land bore witness to some of America's darkest sins—but it also gave rise to some of its most powerful voices. One of those voices is Harriet Tubman.

I took my RV on a pilgrimage south, to Dorchester County, where you'll find the Harriet Tubman Underground Railroad Visitor Center. I walked through the exhibit slowly, reading every word. My chest tightened as I read about the horrific conditions of enslavement. But I felt uplifted too—because here was a woman who refused to be broken.

She didn't just escape—she returned, over and over again, guiding others to freedom through the Underground Railroad. Through woods, swamps, and terror, she chose bravery. Again and again.

Have you ever wondered what you'd risk to do the right thing? What you'd sacrifice to help someone else break free?

Harriet Tubman forces you to ask those questions. And Maryland offers you a space to sit with the answers.

Reginald F. Lewis Museum of Maryland African American History & Culture (Baltimore)

This museum is a beacon. Tucked in the heart of Baltimore, it's not just a collection of artifacts—it's a celebration of resilience, brilliance, and Black excellence.

I walked through galleries that showcased not just the pain of enslavement and segregation, but the joy of culture—music, faith, entrepreneurship, education, and the fight for civil rights. I found myself overwhelmed—angry at injustice, in awe of triumph.

If you think of history as distant or dusty, this museum will change your mind. You'll hear the voices of Black Marylanders past and present, from laborers and freedom fighters to poets, politicians, and athletes.

You'll feel pride that doesn't just belong to one community—it belongs to all of us.

Other Sites of African American and Native American Heritage in Maryland

Banneker-Douglass Museum (Annapolis)

Named for Benjamin Banneker, a Black scientist and astronomer, and Frederick Douglass, the famed abolitionist born in Maryland.

Housed in a historic church, this museum focuses on Black Marylanders' contributions through centuries.

Frederick Douglass Park on the Tuckahoe (Talbot County)

Located near Douglass's birthplace.

A quiet, reverent outdoor park where you can walk, reflect, and imagine the life of a child born into slavery who would one day become one of the most eloquent voices for freedom.

Chesapeake Bay Environmental Center – Native Plant & Heritage Trails Offers insights into indigenous use of natural resources.

Great for those who want to combine history and ecology in a single immersive experience.

RV Campgrounds Near Heritage Sites

These campgrounds give you access not only to comfort, but proximity to some of the most meaningful cultural sites in the state:

Tuckahoe State Park (Near Frederick Douglass Birthplace)

Wooded serenity, biking trails, and easy access to Talbot County's history-rich landscapes.

Greenbelt Park (Near Washington, D.C. & Piscataway Park)

Close to multiple heritage locations while offering peace and quiet in nature.

Piney Point Campground (Southern Maryland)

Excellent base for exploring Native heritage sites and watermen's culture along the Potomac.

Lessons from the Land: What Maryland Teaches Us

Here's the thing about traveling through these places: they don't just tell stories—they make you feel them.

When you visit these sites, you're not just checking off tourist stops. You're honoring lives. You're witnessing strength. You're taking part in the work of remembrance.

And that work is sacred.

So let me ask you:

What stories have you inherited?

What voices do you carry in your heart, even if you've never heard their names?

When you travel with those questions, Maryland becomes more than a destination.
It becomes a reckoning.

A healing.

A promise.

Heritage as a Compass

The past is not behind us—it's beside us.

In Maryland, every shoreline, every forest trail, every museum, and every quiet historic marker is a chance to walk with the people who came before. The Native peoples who revered the land. The enslaved who transformed suffering into strength. The dreamers who built culture out of ashes.

And maybe, as you walk their paths, you'll discover something about your own.

Because if you listen closely—really closely—you'll hear it.

Not just history.

But truth.

CHAPTER 8

MARYLAND'S CULINARY DELIGHTS – CRAB CAKES AND SEAFOOD

The Chesapeake Bay: Maryland's Seafood Heartbeat

Imagine the salty breeze of the Chesapeake Bay kissing your face as you sit down to a plate of golden-brown crab cakes, the centerpiece of Maryland's culinary legacy. The blue crab, native to these waters, is more than just a seafood delicacy—it's a symbol of Maryland's rich maritime heritage. From April to November, the bay teems with these sweet, tender crabs, making it the prime season for indulging in crab dishes. Whether steamed whole with Old Bay seasoning or crafted into succulent crab cakes, the flavors are unparalleled. Maryland's reputation as the "Crab Cake Capital" is well-earned, with its crab cakes being a must-try for any seafood enthusiast.

The Crab Shack: A Kent Island Gem

Nestled on Kent Island, the Stevensville Crab Shack offers an authentic Maryland seafood experience. With the Chesapeake Bay Bridge as a backdrop, diners can savor freshly steamed blue crabs, homemade crab cakes, and other local seafood delights. The family-owned establishment prides itself on quality and tradition, making it a favorite among locals and visitors alike.

Faidley's Seafood: A Baltimore Institution

In the heart of Baltimore's Lexington Market, Faidley's Seafood has been serving up legendary crab cakes since 1886. Known for their jumbo lump crab cakes made with minimal filler, Faidley's has garnered national acclaim, even being featured on the Travel Channel. Their commitment to quality and tradition makes them a must-visit for any seafood lover.

Ocean Odyssey Crab House: A Taste of Tradition

Located in Cambridge, Maryland, Ocean Odyssey Crab House offers a nostalgic dining experience. What began as a crab-picking business in 1947 has evolved into a full-fledged restaurant serving a variety of seafood dishes. Their menu features soups, salads, sandwiches, and seafood by the pound, all prepared with the freshest local ingredients.

RV-Friendly Seafood Stops: Dining on the Go

For those traveling by RV, Maryland offers several seafood establishments that cater to mobile diners. Ocean Odyssey Crab House, located in Cambridge, offers a variety of seafood dishes and is RV-friendly, making it a convenient stop for travelers. Layton's Chance Vineyard and Winery, while primarily a winery, offers RV parking and is located near several seafood restaurants, allowing travelers to enjoy both wine and seafood in one trip.

Crafting the Perfect Maryland Crab Cake at Home

For those inspired to recreate Maryland's iconic crab cakes at home, here's a simple recipe:

Ingredients:

1 lb jumbo lump crab meat

1/4 cup mayonnaise

1 egg

1 tbsp Dijon mustard

1 tsp Old Bay seasoning

1/2 cup crushed saltine crackers

2 tbsp fresh parsley, chopped

Instructions:

In a bowl, combine mayonnaise, egg, mustard, Old Bay seasoning, and parsley.

Gently fold in the crab meat and crushed crackers, being careful not to break up the lumps.

Form the mixture into patties and refrigerate for at least an hour to set.

Heat oil in a skillet over medium heat and cook the patties for 3-4 minutes on each side until golden brown.

Serve with lemon wedges and tartar sauce.

Maryland's culinary scene, particularly its seafood offerings, provides a rich tapestry of flavors and traditions. From the bustling markets of Baltimore to the serene shores of Kent Island, the state's seafood establishments offer something for every palate. Whether you're a seasoned seafood enthusiast or a newcomer eager to explore, Maryland's seafood delights promise an unforgettable dining experience.

FARM-TO-TABLE DINING

Maryland's farm-to-table dining scene is a vibrant, delicious testament to the state's agricultural heritage and its commitment to sustainability. This is where rolling farmlands meet sophisticated kitchens, where local cheesemakers, produce growers, and artisans come together to create food that nourishes both the body and the community. From the bustling streets of Baltimore to the quiet backroads of rural towns, the farm-to-fork movement is thriving—and it's something every food lover traveling through the state should experience.

Have you ever tasted a tomato so fresh it still carries the warmth of the morning sun? Or sampled a cheese that was made just hours earlier on the very farm you're standing on? These aren't rare experiences in Maryland—they're everyday occurrences for those who seek out its authentic farm-to-table culture. For RV travelers and culinary adventurers alike, the state offers an unparalleled opportunity to taste food at its source.

Start in Baltimore, where the city's public markets are treasure troves of local flavor. The Baltimore Farmers' Market & Bazaar, nestled under the Jones Falls Expressway, is the largest producer-only market in Maryland. Here, you'll find everything from organic vegetables and artisanal bread to hand-crafted soaps and heritage meats. The energy is infectious—chefs, families, and foodies mingle among the stalls, sampling goat cheese, locally roasted coffee, and fresh-cut flowers.

From there, head west to Howard County and visit Clark's Elioak Farm, a working family farm that not only offers farm-fresh produce but also a whimsical experience with its Enchanted Forest attractions. Their roadside market features seasonal fruits, jams, local honey, and handmade goods—all part of the farm-to-table fabric that defines Maryland's rural charm.

Venture further into Frederick County, and you'll find a blossoming scene where small-town charm meets serious culinary credibility. Restaurants like The Tasting Room in Frederick source ingredients from local farms daily, offering dishes that shift with the seasons. You might enjoy pan-seared duck breast with sweet potato mash in the fall or heirloom tomato salad with burrata in the summer. These are meals that don't just taste good—they tell a story.

Then there's the experience of dining on the farm itself. In places like Black Ankle Vineyards near Mount Airy, or the multi-generational Prigel Family Creamery in Glen Arm, the table is often just steps away from where your meal began its life. These venues frequently host farm dinners, pairing their offerings with local wines and allowing guests to dine among the vines or beneath twinkling string lights in restored barns.

For RV travelers, Maryland provides ideal ways to enjoy farm-fresh food without sacrificing comfort or convenience. One standout example is the Maple Tree Campground in Rohrersville, near the Antietam Battlefield and several local farms. It's quiet, rustic, and close to seasonal farmers' markets and orchards. In southern Maryland, Greenwell State Park offers RV sites within a short drive of Port of Leonardtown Winery and several farm stands along the scenic byways.

On the Eastern Shore, Tuckahoe State Park provides another RV-friendly haven, located near Easton and its thriving local food scene. At restaurants like Out of the Fire, the chef works directly with nearby growers to craft dishes that are as fresh as they are flavorful. Try their roasted beet salad with goat cheese from a local dairy, and you'll understand why Maryland's farm-to-table movement is gaining such passionate followers.

Have you noticed how different food tastes when you know where it comes from? When you meet the farmer who grew it, or walk the fields where it was harvested? Maryland invites you to slow down and savor those connections. To buy a basket of peaches that were picked just hours ago. To share a conversation with the woman who churned the butter you're spreading on fresh bread. These are the kinds of experiences that turn meals into memories.

In every corner of the state, Maryland's farm-to-table culture reminds us of the value of eating locally and sustainably. It's not just about great food—it's about building relationships, supporting small businesses, and celebrating the land. Whether you're dining at a white-tablecloth restaurant in the city or eating a just-picked apple at a roadside farm stand, you're part of a delicious, grounded tradition.

As you travel, keep your eyes open for signs along the road—"Fresh Eggs," "Farm Store Open Today," "Pick Your Own Strawberries." Pull over. Explore. Talk to the farmers. These detours off the beaten path often lead to the most unforgettable meals of your journey.

BREWERIES AND DISTILLERIES

Maryland's craft beverage scene is nothing short of a revelation. For years, the state quietly nurtured a community of passionate brewers and distillers, but today, it's a full-blown destination for anyone who appreciates the art of fermentation and distillation. The flavors are bold, the creativity boundless, and the commitment to quality unmistakable. If you've never considered Maryland a major player in the world of craft beer and spirits, it's time to look again—and taste.

There's something deeply personal about standing in a taproom, pint in hand, talking to the brewer who poured their heart into that amber ale or citrusy IPA. Have you ever tasted a beer that seemed to perfectly capture the character of the place where it was brewed? That's what Maryland's craft breweries offer—an experience that goes far beyond the glass. Each brewery is a reflection of its surroundings, its people, and its roots.

Take Flying Dog Brewery in Frederick, for instance. Known nationwide for its bold branding and even bolder beers, Flying Dog is a pillar of Maryland's beer scene. From their best-selling Raging Bitch Belgian IPA to seasonal and small-batch brews that push the limits of what beer can be, this is a brewery that refuses to play it safe. Their spacious tasting room and regular events make it a must-visit stop for beer lovers traveling through the western part of the state.

Further east, you'll find the Black Eyed Susan Distillery in Mount Airy, a small-batch operation that crafts everything from smooth vodkas to character-rich bourbons. The name itself is a nod to Maryland's state flower, and the spirits they produce are every bit as local and inspired. Visiting the distillery isn't just about tasting—you'll learn about their process, the locally sourced ingredients, and the care that goes into every bottle. It's a place where tradition meets experimentation, and the results are delicious.

Have you ever planned a trip around a drink? More and more RV travelers are building their itineraries around brewery and distillery stops, and Maryland is especially welcoming to this kind of exploration. The state offers a number of RV-friendly locations that place you right near the action, making it easy to sample the local spirits and safely settle in for the night.

For instance, the Ole Mink Farm Recreation Resort near Frederick provides a comfortable and scenic base just a short drive from several breweries and distilleries, including Flying Dog. This wooded resort offers amenities and full hookups, making it ideal for extended stays. In southern Maryland, Greenwell State Park is not only beautiful but conveniently located for visitors looking to tour regional distilleries and enjoy local tasting rooms.

Closer to the Chesapeake Bay, you'll find RV accommodations near towns like Easton and St. Michaels, which boast their own vibrant beverage scenes. Lyons Distillery in St. Michaels is known for its craft rum and gin, while Eastern Shore Brewing is a staple for small-batch beer fans. These spots often host events, live music, and community festivals, offering more than just a drink—they provide a taste of Maryland's culture.

What sets Maryland apart isn't just the quality of its beer and spirits, but the authenticity behind them. These are people rooted in their communities, using local ingredients, collaborating with nearby farms, and investing in sustainable practices. Every sip tells a story—of the soil, the seasons, and the spirit of the people who live here.

The state's Craft Beverage Trail offers a roadmap for those wanting to dive deeper, connecting breweries and distilleries across Maryland. It's an invitation to explore not just what's in your glass, but how it got there, and why it matters. Whether you're raising a glass in a modern, industrial-style taproom or sipping whiskey in a converted barn, you're experiencing Maryland's commitment to craft.

So, as you plan your culinary tour of Maryland, don't overlook its liquid treasures. From hoppy IPAs and barrel-aged stouts to botanical gins and farm-crafted rye, there's a world of flavor waiting. Whether you're sampling at the source or bringing a bottle back to your RV to enjoy under the stars, Maryland's breweries and distilleries promise to elevate your journey in ways you won't forget.

CHAPTER 9

RV SAFETY AND MAINTENANCE IN MARYLAND

NAVIGATING MARYLAND'S ROADS SAFELY

Embarking on an RV journey through Maryland offers a tapestry of experiences—from the rolling hills of the western mountains to the serene shores of the Chesapeake Bay. Yet, as exhilarating as it is, driving an RV in Maryland presents unique challenges. The state's diverse terrain, coupled with its bustling urban centers and narrow coastal roads, demands heightened awareness and preparation.

Conquering Maryland's Hilly Terrain

The western part of Maryland, particularly the Appalachian region, boasts picturesque landscapes. However, these areas also present steep inclines and winding roads that can be daunting for RV drivers. I recall my first ascent through the Allegheny Mountains; the engine labored, and my knuckles whitened on the steering wheel. The sheer drop-offs on the side were enough to make one's heart race.

To navigate these terrains safely:

Shift to Lower Gears: This reduces engine strain and provides better control on descents.

Use Engine Braking: Instead of relying solely on brakes, use engine braking to maintain a safe speed downhill, preventing brake overheating.

Monitor Temperature Gauges: Steep climbs can cause engines to overheat. Regularly check temperature gauges and pull over if necessary to let the engine cool.

Avoid Overloading: Ensure your RV's weight is within recommended limits. Overloading can affect braking efficiency and stability.

Maneuvering Narrow Coastal Roads

The eastern shore of Maryland, with its charming towns and coastal views, offers narrow roads that can be challenging for RVs. I vividly remember squeezing through the tight streets of St. Michaels, with barely an inch to spare on either side. The proximity of parked cars and pedestrians added to the tension.

Tips for navigating these roads:

Drive During Off-Peak Hours: Early mornings or weekdays often have less traffic, providing more room to maneuver.

Utilize Spotters: If possible, have a co-pilot assist by guiding you through tight spots.

Practice in Open Areas: Before venturing into narrow streets, practice your RV's turning radius in open parking lots.

Stay Calm and Patient: Rushing can lead to mistakes. Take your time and ensure every turn is deliberate.

Navigating Urban Areas

Cities like Baltimore and Annapolis present their own set of challenges. Congested traffic, tight parking spaces, and unfamiliar road signs can overwhelm even seasoned RV drivers. I once found myself circling Baltimore's Inner Harbor, searching for a place to park, only to realize that RVs were prohibited in most garages.

Strategies for urban RV driving:

Research Parking Options: Before entering a city, research RV-friendly parking areas or campgrounds nearby.

Avoid City Centers: Whenever possible, park outside the city and use public transportation or ride-sharing services to reach your destination.

Stay Informed About Regulations: Each city may have different rules regarding RVs. Ensure you're aware of any restrictions or permits required.

Best Apps for Navigation and Real-Time Traffic Updates

In today's digital age, several apps can assist RV drivers in Maryland:

Google Maps: Offers real-time traffic updates, turn-by-turn navigation, and offline maps. It's invaluable for urban driving and provides Street View to preview routes.

Waze: A community-driven app that provides real-time alerts about accidents, road closures, and police presence. Its dynamic routing can help avoid traffic jams.

RV LIFE App: Tailored for RVers, this app offers route planning based on RV dimensions, campground locator, and offline maps.

Maryland Roads Traffic App: Provides live traffic reports, video feeds, and incident alerts specific to Maryland.

RV Road Safety Advice for Tourists Driving During Peak Seasons

Maryland's peak tourist seasons, especially spring and summer, see an influx of RV travelers. While the scenic beauty is a major draw, the increased traffic and crowded attractions can pose risks.

Preparing for Peak Season Challenges

During my trip to Assateague Island in July, I encountered long lines at the entrance and limited parking spaces. The excitement of the wild horses was overshadowed by the stress of finding a spot for my RV.

To mitigate such challenges:

Book Campgrounds in Advance: Popular spots like Assateague and Deep Creek Lake fill up quickly. Reserve your spot months ahead.

Arrive Early: Aim to reach popular destinations early in the day to secure parking and avoid the midday rush.

Stay Informed About Events: Major events can cause road closures and heavy traffic. Check local event calendars before planning your route.

Understanding Seasonal Road Conditions

Maryland's weather can be unpredictable. Winters bring icy roads, while summers can cause pavement softening, especially on rural routes. I once drove through a rural road in the summer heat, only to find the asphalt softening under my RV's weight, causing a bumpy ride.

Tips for varying road conditions:

Check Weather Forecasts: Before traveling, check weather conditions to anticipate any road hazards.

Avoid Driving During Extreme Heat: If possible, avoid driving during the hottest parts of the day to prevent road damage.

Be Cautious on Bridges: Bridges can freeze before roadways. Exercise extra caution during winter months.

Tips for Safe RV Driving in Maryland

Safety should always be a priority. Reflecting on my experiences:

Regularly Inspect Your RV: Before each journey, check tire pressure, fluid levels, and brakes.

Stay Within Speed Limits: RVs take longer to stop. Adhering to speed limits ensures you have ample time to react.

Maintain a Safe Following Distance: This provides enough space to maneuver and react to sudden stops.

Driving an RV through Maryland is an adventure filled with diverse landscapes and rich history. However, it requires preparation, awareness, and adaptability. By understanding the unique challenges Maryland's roads present and utilizing the right tools and strategies, you can ensure a safe and enjoyable journey.

Remember, every twist and turn is an opportunity to create lasting memories. Embrace the journey, stay informed, and drive safely.

MAINTAINING YOUR RV WHILE ON THE ROAD IN MARYLAND

Embarking on an RV journey through Maryland is an exhilarating adventure. From the bustling streets of Baltimore to the serene landscapes of the Eastern Shore, the state offers a diverse array of experiences for RV travelers. However, to ensure your journey remains smooth and enjoyable, it's imperative to maintain your RV in top condition. This chapter delves into preventive maintenance tips, highlights reputable RV service centers across Maryland, and provides guidance on assembling an emergency kit tailored to Maryland's unique climate and road conditions.

Preventive Maintenance: The Key to a Trouble-Free Journey

Imagine cruising down the scenic Route 50, the sun setting over the Chesapeake Bay, when suddenly, your RV's engine sputters and comes to a halt. The serenity is shattered, and the dream trip turns into a stressful ordeal. This scenario underscores the importance of preventive maintenance.

1. Regular Engine Checks

Before hitting the road, always inspect your engine. Ensure oil levels are adequate, belts are tensioned correctly, and there are no visible leaks. Regular oil changes are crucial for engine longevity.

2. Tire Maintenance

Your RV's tires bear the brunt of the journey. Check tire pressure before each trip, inspect for wear and tear, and ensure they are properly aligned. Uneven tire wear can lead to handling issues and increased fuel consumption.

3. Brake System Inspection

Given the added weight of an RV, brakes are under significant stress. Regularly inspect brake pads and discs for wear. Listen for unusual noises when braking, as they can indicate potential issues.

4. Plumbing and Water Systems

Ensure all water lines are free from leaks. In colder months, winterize your RV to prevent freezing pipes. Regularly flush the water system to prevent buildup and ensure clean water supply.

5. Electrical System Checks

Inspect all electrical connections, including batteries, fuses, and wiring. Ensure that all lights, appliances, and outlets are functioning correctly.

RV Service Centers Across Maryland

When preventive maintenance isn't enough, or if you encounter unexpected issues, it's essential to know where to turn for professional assistance. Here are some reputable RV service centers across Maryland:

1. Queenstown RV & Marine Center

Located in College Park, Queenstown RV offers comprehensive services, including collision repair and routine maintenance.

2. MidAtlantic RV Service

Situated in Edgewood, this facility provides a range of services from roof repairs to appliance installations.

3. Maryland Auto & Truck Repair

Based in Glen Burnie, they offer services like engine diagnostics, brake replacements, and AC servicing.

4. Superior Auto Service Center

In Frederick, they specialize in RV-specific services, including fluid system checks and air conditioning maintenance.

5. Cranberry Auto Service Center

Located in Westminster, they focus on addressing common RV issues like water leaks and electrical problems.

Assembling an Emergency Kit for Maryland's Climate and Roads

Maryland's diverse climate and road conditions necessitate a well-equipped emergency kit. Here's a comprehensive list tailored to the state's unique challenges:

1. Basic Tools

Multi-tool or Swiss Army Knife: Versatile for various repairs.

Duct Tape and Electrical Tape: For temporary fixes.

Screwdrivers and Wrenches: Essential for mechanical adjustments.

Pliers and Wire Cutters: Useful for electrical issues.

2. Tire Repair Kit

Tire Pressure Gauge: To monitor tire pressure.

Tire Sealant: For quick fixes of minor punctures.

Portable Air Compressor: To inflate tires on the go.

3. Electrical Supplies

Fuses and Circuit Breakers: To replace blown fuses.

Battery Jumper Cables: For jump-starting a dead battery.

Portable Power Bank: To charge devices in emergencies.

4. Plumbing Essentials

Water Pump: For water system issues.

Plumbing Tape and Sealant: To address leaks. **Water Filter**: To ensure clean water supply.

5. Safety Items

First Aid Kit: For medical emergencies.

Fire Extinguisher: To combat small fires.

Reflective Triangles or Flares: To alert other drivers in case of a breakdown.

Flashlight with Extra Batteries: For visibility during nighttime issues.

6. Maryland-Specific Considerations

Sun Protection: Sunscreen and hats for hot summer days.

Rain Gear: Ponchos and umbrellas for sudden showers.

Cold Weather Gear: Blankets and warm clothing for unexpected cold snaps.

Maintaining your RV while on the road in Maryland requires diligence, preparation, and the right resources. By adhering to preventive maintenance practices, knowing where to seek professional help, and being equipped with a comprehensive emergency kit, you can ensure a safe and enjoyable journey through the Old Line State. Remember, the road ahead is full of possibilities—be prepared to embrace them all.

WEATHER AND SEASONAL CONSIDERATIONS FOR RV TRAVEL IN MARYLAND

Maryland may be a small state, but it delivers big when it comes to seasonal variety. If you've ever sat in your RV on a humid July afternoon in Ocean City, sweating through your clothes, or tried to start your engine after an unexpected December freeze in the mountains near Deep Creek Lake, you know firsthand—Maryland's weather can be *unforgiving* if you're unprepared.

Traveling through Maryland in an RV means dancing with every season, and if you're not ready, each one has its own way of testing you. In this chapter, I'll share personal stories, hard-earned lessons, and real strategies to help you master Maryland's wild swings in climate and get the best out of every season. From melting tires on summer pavement to winterized tanks that refused to thaw—I've lived through the chaos so you don't have to.

Maryland's Climate in a Nutshell

Maryland's location in the Mid-Atlantic region gives it a four-season climate. Here's a general breakdown:

Summer (June–August): Hot and humid, especially in the eastern and southern regions.

Fall (September–November): Crisp air, stunning foliage, and cooler temperatures.

Winter (December–February): Snow in the west, cold rains and frost elsewhere.

Spring (March–May): Wet and warming up, with flowers blooming and rivers swelling.

Each season offers something different for RV travelers—but also its own set of maintenance concerns, driving hazards, and lifestyle adjustments.

RVing in Maryland's Summer Heat

Let me paint you a picture: it's late July, and I'm parked near Assateague Island. The sun's blaring, the AC's running on overdrive, and I swear the walls of my RV were sweating. The coastal breeze? Nowhere to be found.

Challenges:

Overheating engines and appliances.

Strain on AC systems.

Increased tire pressure from road heat.

Humidity-related mold and mildew.

Tips:

Check coolant levels frequently and monitor engine temperature.

Install reflective window shades to keep heat out.

Park in shaded areas and use awnings strategically.

Ventilate your RV early in the day and late in the evening.

Use dehumidifiers or moisture absorbers to prevent mold.

Pro Tip: Avoid driving during the hottest part of the day—typically 1 to 5 p.m. Instead, plan activities or rest during that window and hit the road earlier or later.

Fall: The Golden Season for RV Travel

Fall in Maryland is spectacular. I still remember driving along Skyline Drive, the leaves glowing in every shade of red and gold, my windows cracked to let in the crisp breeze. There's a peaceful magic to it.

Benefits:

Cooler temperatures make for comfortable travel.

Lighter tourist traffic.

Fall foliage in western Maryland is breathtaking.

Considerations:

Shorter daylight hours require more careful planning.

Morning frost can become a concern by late October.

Leaf-covered roads can be slippery.

Tips:

Check your RV's heating system and test your furnace before it gets cold.

Carry a heated hose or insulated hose wrap—fall nights can freeze in western Maryland.

Layer clothing so you're always prepared for a shift in temperature.

Surviving Maryland's Winter in an RV

RVing in winter? In Maryland? Believe it or not, it can be done—and can be rewarding. I once spent a December week near Deep Creek Lake, with a heater running, snow falling gently outside, and hot cocoa steaming on the stove. It was *magical*, but also *risky*.

Challenges:

Freezing pipes and water tanks.

Black ice and snow-covered roads.

Limited campground availability.

Must-Do Winter Prep:

Winterize water lines with antifreeze or use heated hose systems.

Install skirting around the RV to keep cold air out from beneath.

Use propane heaters (with CO2 detectors installed) or electric space heaters safely.

Keep a shovel and de-icer handy at all times.

Driving Tips:

Check weather and road conditions constantly.

Keep tire chains in your emergency kit.

Drive slower and avoid steep inclines when roads are icy.

Springtime: When the RV Season Awakens

Spring brings mud, moisture, and mayhem—but also the promise of renewal. There's something energizing about a spring RV trip in Maryland, even if it means dealing with the occasional thunderstorm.

What to Expect:

Unpredictable weather—sunny one day, downpour the next.

Flooded backroads and muddy campgrounds.

Blooming wildflowers and increasing wildlife activity.

Spring Travel Tips:

Inspect seals and roofing for leaks after winter storage.

Check your batteries—cold weather can drain them.

Watch out for wet roads and standing water—especially in rural or low-lying areas.

Keep extra towels and waterproof mats at the RV entrance to manage mud.

The Best Months for RV Travel in Maryland

Not all months are created equal—some bring joy, others bring chaos.

Best Months (for comfort, safety, and experiences):

May: Mild weather, blooming landscapes, fewer crowds.

September: Warm days, cool nights, lower humidity.

October: Fall colors, harvest festivals, and ideal travel temps.

Tricky Months:

July & August: Hot, humid, and heavy tourist traffic.

January & February: Snowstorms in the west and icy rain in the east.

Questions to Ask Yourself Before Each Season

To keep your travels smooth and enjoyable, ask:

Is my RV equipped for the temperature extremes of this season?

Are there seasonal events or road closures that might impact my trip?

Do I need to modify my packing list—clothing, tools, or maintenance supplies?

How does this season affect campground availability and accessibility?

Maryland is beautiful year-round, but each season demands respect and preparation. When you plan accordingly, the state opens up like a well-written novel—layered, compelling, and full of memorable chapters. Whether you're chasing fireflies on a summer night near the Chesapeake or watching snowfall on a quiet mountain ridge, Maryland will meet you where you are—*if you're ready for it.*

So, what season will you choose for your next RV journey?

CHAPTER 10

HIDDEN GEMS AND OFF-THE-BEATEN-PATH ADVENTURES

EXPLORING MARYLAND'S SMALL TOWNS AND VILLAGES

The Allure of the Road Less Traveled

Have you ever felt the magnetic pull of a place that whispers secrets of history, culture, and charm? A place where time slows down, allowing you to breathe deeply and savor the moment? That's the essence of Maryland's small towns and villages—hidden gems waiting to be discovered. In this chapter, we embark on a journey through three such towns: St. Michaels, Berlin, and Sharpsburg. Each offers a unique tapestry of experiences, from antique shopping and local dining to rich historical sites and cozy RV parks.

St. Michaels: A Maritime Haven

The Charm of St. Michaels

Nestled on the Eastern Shore, St. Michaels is a picturesque town with a rich maritime heritage. Its historic district, added to the National Register of Historic Places in 1986, boasts 19th-century architecture and a vibrant waterfront. Walking through Talbot Street feels like stepping back in time, with boutique shops, art galleries, and cafes lining the streets. The town's transformation from a shipbuilding hub to a tourist destination has preserved its old-world charm while embracing modern amenities.

Must-Visit Attractions

Chesapeake Bay Maritime Museum: This 18-acre museum offers interactive exhibits on the region's maritime history. Visitors can explore historic vessels, including the National Historic Landmark *Edna E. Lockwood*, and learn about the Chesapeake Bay's ecology and heritage .

St. Michaels Museum: Located at St. Mary's Square, this museum delves into the town's 19th-century history, offering walking tours that provide insights into the lives of early residents .

Historic District: The heart of St. Michaels, the Historic District is perfect for leisurely strolls, offering a glimpse into the town's past through its well-preserved architecture and quaint shops.

RV Parks in St. Michaels

For those traveling by RV, St. Michaels offers several options:

St. Michaels RV Park: Located near the town center, this park provides easy access to local attractions and the waterfront.

Camp Merryelande: Situated a short drive from St. Michaels, this campground offers a peaceful retreat with amenities like fishing spots and nature trails.

Berlin: A Blend of History and Modernity

Discovering Berlin

Just 10 miles from the Atlantic Ocean, Berlin is a town that seamlessly blends its rich history with contemporary flair. Recognized by *Coastal Living Magazine* as one of America's Top Ten Romantic Escapes in 2007, Berlin's charm lies in its preserved 19th-century architecture and vibrant arts scene . Walking through its streets feels like exploring a living museum, with each building telling a story of the past.

Highlights of Berlin

Historic District: Listed on the National Register of Historic Places, Berlin's downtown area is a testament to its storied past. The architecture reflects Georgian, Federal, and Gothic Revival styles, offering a visual feast for history enthusiasts.

Antique Shops and Art Galleries: Berlin is a haven for antique lovers and art aficionados. The town boasts numerous antique shops and galleries, showcasing everything from vintage furniture to contemporary art.

Local Dining: The culinary scene in Berlin is diverse, with restaurants offering everything from classic American fare to international cuisines. Dining here is an experience, with many establishments housed in historic buildings, adding to the ambiance.

RV Parks Near Berlin

Shore Point Cottages: Located on Stephen Decatur Highway, this campground offers 52 rental cottages and RV sites. Amenities include a swimming pool, laundry facilities, and a dog park, making it a comfortable base for exploring Berlin and the surrounding areas .

Sun Outdoors Ocean City: Situated in Berlin, this RV resort provides a range of amenities, including a fitness center, miniature golf, and a tiki bar. It's just a short drive from Ocean City, allowing guests to enjoy both the tranquility of Berlin and the excitement of the beach.

Sharpsburg: A Step Back in Time

The Significance of Sharpsburg

Sharpsburg is a town steeped in history, most notably as the site of the Battle of Antietam during the American Civil War. The Antietam National Battlefield, located just north of the town, commemorates this pivotal battle . The town itself is listed on the National Register of Historic Places, with structures dating back to the 18th century, offering a glimpse into early American life.

Exploring Sharpsburg

Antietam National Battlefield: Visitors can tour the battlefield, visit the visitor center, and pay respects at the national cemetery. The site offers a profound insight into the events of the Civil War and its impact on the nation.

Sharpsburg Historic District: The town's historic district features buildings in Georgian, Federal, and Gothic Revival styles. Walking through its streets provides a sense of the town's evolution over the centuries.

Memorial Day Commemoration: Sharpsburg hosts one of the nation's longest-running Memorial Day celebrations, honoring those who served in the military. The event includes ceremonies, parades, and community gatherings, reflecting the town's deep respect for its history and heritage.

RV Parks Near Sharpsburg

Antietam Creek Campground: Located just outside Sharpsburg, this campground offers RV sites with full hookups, along with amenities like a swimming pool and fishing areas. It's an ideal spot for those wishing to explore the battlefield and the surrounding countryside.

Hagerstown City Park Campground: A short drive from Sharpsburg, this campground provides a peaceful setting with access to hiking trails and picnic areas, perfect for nature lovers.

Tips for Exploring Maryland's Small Towns

Plan Ahead: While these towns are charming, some attractions may have limited hours or seasonal availability. Check ahead to ensure you don't miss out.

Support Local Businesses: Dining at locally-owned restaurants and shopping at independent stores helps sustain the unique character of these towns.

Respect History: Many of these towns have rich historical backgrounds. Take time to learn about their past and appreciate the preservation efforts.

Pack Accordingly: Depending on the season, weather can vary. Bring layers and be prepared for changing conditions.

The Magic of Small Towns

Exploring Maryland's small towns offers more than just a getaway; it provides an opportunity to connect with history, culture, and community. Whether you're strolling through the historic streets of St. Michaels, browsing the antique shops of Berlin, or reflecting on the past in Sharpsburg, each town has a story to tell. So, pack your bags, hit the road, and uncover the hidden gems of Maryland's small towns. The adventure awaits.

UNDERRATED NATURE ESCAPES IN MARYLAND

Seeking Solitude in Nature

Have you ever longed for a place where the only sounds are the rustling of leaves, the call of a distant bird, and the gentle flow of a river? A place where the hustle and bustle of daily life fade into the background, and you're left with nothing but the serenity of nature? Maryland, often overshadowed by its bustling cities, harbors hidden natural sanctuaries that offer just that. In this chapter, we delve into two such gems: Pocomoke River State Park and the Western Maryland Rail Trail. These locales provide unparalleled opportunities for hiking, birdwatching, and immersing oneself in the tranquility of the outdoors.

Pocomoke River State Park: A Tranquil Retreat

A Haven for Nature Enthusiasts

Located on Maryland's Eastern Shore, Pocomoke River State Park is a haven for those seeking solitude amidst nature's embrace. The park's diverse ecosystems, ranging from tidal wetlands to ancient forests, make it a prime spot for wildlife observation and outdoor recreation.

Birdwatching Paradise: The Pocomoke River Wildlife Management Area (WMA), encompassing parts of the state park, is renowned for its birdwatching opportunities. It's home to various species, including hawks, osprey, and bald eagles .

Hiking Trails: The park offers several trails suitable for hiking. The Shad Landing Area features nearly 3 miles of trails, including the Trail of Change, which showcases the area's ecological transformations over time .

Canoeing and Kayaking: The Pocomoke River provides calm waters ideal for canoeing and kayaking. Rentals are available in nearby towns like Snow Hill, allowing visitors to explore the river's winding path through lush landscapes.

Camping: For those wishing to extend their stay, the park offers various camping options. The Mattaponi Ponds Camping Area provides backcountry campsites, offering a more secluded experience .

Tips for Visiting

Best Time to Visit: Spring and fall offer mild temperatures and vibrant foliage, enhancing the park's beauty.

Wildlife Etiquette: Maintain a respectful distance from wildlife and refrain from feeding animals to preserve their natural behaviors.

Preparation: Bring insect repellent, especially during warmer months, as mosquitoes can be prevalent.

Western Maryland Rail Trail: A Journey Through History and Nature

A Scenic Pathway

The Western Maryland Rail Trail (WMRT) stretches approximately 28 miles, paralleling the C&O Canal and the Potomac River. This paved trail, reclaimed from the former Western Maryland Railway, offers a unique blend of natural beauty and historical significance.

Historical Landmarks: Along the trail, visitors can encounter remnants of the past, including old railway structures and interpretive signs detailing the area's history.

Wildlife Observation: The trail's diverse habitats support various wildlife species. Birdwatchers can spot numerous species, and the surrounding forests and wetlands are home to deer, foxes, and other animals.

Accessibility: The trail's flat, paved surface makes it accessible for all ages and abilities. It's suitable for walking, biking, and inline skating.

Scenic Views: The trail offers breathtaking views of the Potomac River, especially during sunrise and sunset, providing perfect opportunities for photography.

Tips for Visiting

Trailheads: Popular starting points include Hancock Station and Big Pool Station, both offering ample parking and access to the trail.

Amenities: While the trail is equipped with basic amenities, it's advisable to bring water, snacks, and sun protection, as services along the trail can be limited.

Respect the Environment: Stay on designated paths to protect the surrounding flora and fauna.

Hidden Campgrounds for Peace and Quiet

For those seeking solitude away from crowded campsites, Maryland offers several lesser-known campgrounds that provide a peaceful retreat.

Green Ridge State Forest: Located in western Maryland, this forest offers dispersed camping opportunities amidst its 50+ miles of trails. It's an ideal spot for those seeking solitude and a deeper connection with nature .

Paw Paw Tunnel Campground: Situated near the scenic C&O Canal, this small campground offers a peaceful and secluded camping experience. Campers can explore the nearby Paw Paw Tunnel and enjoy hiking, biking, and fishing opportunities .

Janes Island State Park: Tucked away on Maryland's Eastern Shore, Janes Island State Park offers a unique camping experience surrounded by salt marshes and tidal rivers. It's a haven for kayakers and those seeking a tranquil environment .

Tips for Finding Hidden Campgrounds

Research: Utilize resources like the Maryland Department of Natural Resources website and local outdoor forums to discover lesser-known campgrounds.

Reservations: While some hidden campgrounds operate on a first-come, first-served basis, it's advisable to make reservations when possible, especially during peak seasons.

Preparation: Many secluded campgrounds lack modern amenities. Ensure you're well-prepared with necessary supplies, including water, food, and camping gear.

Embracing Maryland's Natural Beauty

Maryland's underrated nature escapes offer a sanctuary for those seeking peace, solitude, and a deeper connection with the environment. Whether it's hiking the tranquil trails of Pocomoke River State Park, cycling along the scenic Western Maryland Rail Trail, or camping in hidden gems like Green Ridge State Forest, these locales provide an opportunity to disconnect from the chaos of daily life and immerse oneself in the serenity of nature.

So, the next time you yearn for an escape, consider venturing into Maryland's lesser-known natural sanctuaries. The beauty and tranquility await.

QUIRKY ATTRACTIONS AND ROADSIDE WONDERS IN MARYLAND

Embracing the Unconventional

Have you ever found yourself cruising down a scenic highway, only to spot a towering statue or an unexpected roadside attraction that makes you do a double-take? Those are the moments that transform a regular road trip into an unforgettable adventure. Maryland, with its rich history and vibrant culture, is home to a plethora of quirky attractions that are often overlooked by the typical tourist. In this chapter, we delve into some of these hidden gems, from spiritual sanctuaries to colossal crustaceans, and explore how you can experience them in the comfort of your RV.

The National Shrine Grotto of Our Lady of Lourdes: A Spiritual Retreat in the Mountains

Nestled in the serene hills of Emmitsburg, the National Shrine Grotto of Our Lady of Lourdes offers a peaceful escape from the hustle and bustle of everyday life. Established in 1875, it is the oldest replica of the Lourdes shrine in France and serves as a place of prayer and pilgrimage. The grotto features a stunning golden statue of the Blessed Mother, visible for miles around, and a series of peaceful pathways adorned with statues and shrines. Visitors can light candles, meditate in the tranquil surroundings, and collect blessed water from the natural spring on-site.

RV-Friendly Accommodations Nearby:

Emmitsburg Campground: Located just a short drive from the grotto, this campground offers full-hookup sites suitable for RVs. Guests can enjoy amenities like picnic tables, fire rings, and access to hiking trails.

Mountain View RV Park: Situated in nearby Thurmont, this park provides spacious sites with scenic views of the surrounding mountains. It's an ideal base for exploring both the grotto and the nearby Catoctin Mountain Park.

The World's Largest Maryland Crab: A Monument to Local Heritage

In the heart of Crisfield, Maryland, stands a colossal blue crab sculpture that pays homage to the region's rich seafood heritage. This oversized crustacean, crafted from metal and painted in vibrant colors, serves as a whimsical reminder of the area's thriving crab industry. While it may not hold an official world record, the sculpture has become a beloved landmark for both locals and visitors.

Nearby Attractions and Activities:

Crisfield Heritage Foundation: Learn about the town's history and maritime culture through exhibits and guided tours.

Crisfield City Dock: Take a leisurely stroll along the waterfront, enjoy fresh seafood at local eateries, and watch the boats come and go.

RV-Friendly Accommodations:

Somers Cove Marina: Offers RV sites with full hookups and easy access to the waterfront. Guests can enjoy fishing, kayaking, and scenic views of the harbor.

Fort Smallwood Park: A Historic Fortress Overlooking the Bay

Perched on a peninsula where the Patapsco River meets the Chesapeake Bay, Fort Smallwood Park in Pasadena, Maryland, offers a unique blend of history and natural beauty. Established in 1928, the park features the remnants of a historic fort, including Battery Hartshorne, which once served as a coastal defense during World War II. Today, visitors can explore the fort's structures, enjoy picnicking areas, and take in panoramic views of the bay.

RV-Friendly Accommodations Nearby:

Sandy Point State Park: Located just across the bay, this park offers RV sites with water and electric hookups. Guests can enjoy beach access, fishing, and hiking trails.

Tips for Exploring Maryland's Quirky Attractions in Your RV

Plan Ahead: While many of these attractions are open year-round, it's always a good idea to check their websites or contact them directly for current hours and any special events.

Pack Accordingly: Some sites, like the National Shrine Grotto, involve walking on uneven terrain. Wear comfortable shoes and bring essentials like water, sunscreen, and a hat.

Respect Local Customs: Many of these attractions are in small communities with rich traditions. Be mindful of local customs and always ask for permission before taking photographs, especially in religious or cultural sites.

Embracing the Unconventional

Maryland's quirky attractions offer a delightful detour from the typical tourist path. Whether you're seeking spiritual solace at the National Shrine Grotto, marveling at the giant crab in Crisfield, or exploring the historic fort at Fort Smallwood Park, these unique sites provide memorable experiences that enrich your journey. So, next time you're planning a road trip, consider veering off the beaten path and discovering the charm of Maryland's roadside wonders.

CHAPTER 11

SEASONAL RV ADVENTURES IN MARYLAND – SUMMER FESTIVALS AND EVENTS

WHEN THE OPEN ROAD MEETS SUMMER MAGIC

I still remember the first time I rolled into Maryland during the summer in my weathered RV. The sun was high, cicadas singing in the background, and the smell of funnel cake and BBQ was thick in the air. I had no concrete plan—just a vague idea that Maryland was home to some quirky summer festivals. Little did I know, I was about to stumble into a whirlwind of color, sound, and community spirit that would keep calling me back year after year.

Have you ever felt like the universe was trying to get your attention? Like no matter where you go, something extraordinary is just around the corner—but only if you're willing to chase it down? That's what RVing through Maryland in the summer felt like. Every curve in the road led me to something unexpected: a jazz band playing in a tiny waterfront town, a firework show exploding over Chesapeake Bay, or a medieval reenactment in a forest clearing that made me feel like I'd time-traveled.

This chapter is for the curious traveler. The one who craves not just destinations, but experiences—who wants to taste the crab cakes, dance with locals under string lights, and wake up next to a lake with music still echoing in the trees.

If that sounds like you, keep reading. Because Maryland's summer festivals are more than events—they're adventures waiting to happen.

Section 1: Why Maryland in Summer? A Hidden Gem for RV Travelers

Maryland is a small state with a big heart. Tucked between bustling metros and coastal calm, it's the kind of place that surprises you. Summers here are vibrant, often overlooked in favor of nearby beach towns or big cities. But if you're in an RV, Maryland transforms into a living map of festivities—each one with its own flavor, crowd, and rhythm.

Why it Works for RVers:

Compact geography: You can hit multiple festivals in a week without long drives.

Diverse landscapes: From mountain fairs in western Maryland to seafood festivals by the bay.

Well-equipped parks: Plenty of campgrounds tailored to travelers during festival season.

Ask yourself:

Have you ever wondered why some summer trips feel forgettable while others burn into your memory? Could it be the people, the spontaneity, or just the perfect mix of music, food, and fresh air?

Section 2: Top Summer Festivals That Belong on Your RV Bucket List

1. The Maryland State Fair – Timonium

Late August – Early September

The crown jewel of summer events. Think: Ferris wheels, horse races, livestock shows, and fried everything.

What Makes It Special:

Live concerts from major acts

Kids' zones and agricultural exhibitions

Traditional fairgrounds atmosphere with a modern twist

Where to Park Your RV:

Merry Meadows Recreation Farm – 20 minutes away with full hookups, trails, and shade.

Pro Tip: Arrive midweek for fewer crowds and better RV site availability.

2. Artscape – Baltimore

Mid-July

Claimed as America's largest free arts festival, Artscape turns Baltimore into a street museum of installations, performances, and handmade goods.

What Makes It Special:

Over 100 visual artists on display

Live music from local and international acts

Food trucks galore and interactive exhibits

RV Stay Recommendation:

Cherry Hill Park – Full-service, safe, and just a short drive from downtown via public transit.

Trigger Question:

When was the last time you got lost—in the best way—among art that made you stop and *feel* something?

3. **National Hard Crab Derby – Crisfield**

Labor Day Weekend

Celebrate Maryland's seafood soul in Crisfield with boat races, crab cooking contests, and yes—crab races.

What Makes It Special:

The quirky crab races

Fireworks over the bay

Blue crab feasts and live beach music

Nearby RV Camping:

Janes Island State Park – Waterfront sites, kayaking trails, and stunning sunsets.

4. **Columbia Festival of the Arts**

Early June

Spread across several weeks, this festival in Columbia offers everything from open-air jazz concerts to indie film screenings.

Best For: Travelers who enjoy a quieter, more cultured pace.

RV Park Tip:

Little Bennett Campground – Peaceful, wooded, and close to Columbia.

Section 3: Planning the Ultimate Festival-Focused RV Trip

Creating a Custom Festival Route

Combine rural fairs and city festivals for a dynamic trip

Build in rest days between events for recovery and reflection

Pre-book RV spots 3-6 months in advance during peak season

Sample 10-Day Itinerary:

Day 1–2: Columbia Festival of the Arts

Day 3–5: Artscape, Baltimore

Day 6: Rest by the Chesapeake

Day 7–10: Maryland State Fair + Crab Derby

Section 4: Festival Hacks Only Experienced RVers Know

Logistics & Tips

Always check if festivals have RV parking or shuttle services

Arrive early or late to avoid tight parking jams

Keep a foldable bike or scooter for quick access to events

Food & Comfort

Pack a cooler for leftovers (you *will* have some)

Bring earplugs—festivals can go well into the night

Shade tents are lifesavers during day events

Section 5: Real Moments on the Road – My Summer of Surprises

It was at the National Hard Crab Derby that I first danced barefoot with strangers on a dock as fireworks lit up the bay. I didn't plan to be there. I only stopped in Crisfield because my original campground was full. Isn't that how the best memories are made?

I've learned something important from these Maryland festivals: sometimes, you don't need a destination. You need a direction. And maybe a lobster roll.

Don't Just Travel—Celebrate

Maryland's summer isn't just a season. It's a feeling. A blend of tradition and thrill, hometown charm and spontaneous celebration. Whether you're looking for connection, curiosity, or just a damn good crab cake—this is where you'll find it.

So, pack your lawn chair, tune your playlist, and hit the road.

Are you ready to let summer find you?

AUTUMN FOLIAGE AND HARVEST ACTIVITIES IN MARYLAND

The Season That Changed Everything

I didn't know it then, but that October was going to shift something inside me.

I was somewhere along Route 40 in Western Maryland, windows down, a soft flannel blanket draped over my lap. The wind had that unmistakable bite of fall, and the trees—God, the trees—were on fire. Not in a dangerous way, but in that breathtaking, burnished amber-and-ruby way that only autumn can manage. I remember pulling over on a narrow scenic turnout, not because I needed gas or food, but because I had to feel it. I needed to sit still and let the moment soak in.

Have you ever had a season reach into your chest and squeeze your heart? Have you ever looked at a line of maple trees and felt like they were saying something—something you couldn't quite put into words?

That's what fall in Maryland did to me.

This chapter is more than a travel guide—it's a reflection of how the harvest season speaks to our deepest selves. Whether you're seeking peace among falling leaves or joy in a pumpkin-stained smile, let this journey through Maryland's autumn awaken something in you, too.

Section 1: Why Fall in Maryland Feels Like Coming Home

The Heartbeat of the Season

Maryland's fall is a brief, brilliant moment. It doesn't shout; it whispers. It nudges. It invites.

What makes it magical?

Crisp mountain air and Appalachian overlooks

Cider-sweet mornings and flannel-soft evenings

Fields turned golden and forests aflame with color

Unlike other states where autumn fades quickly, Maryland offers layers—coastal calm, mid-state charm, and western wilderness—each turning color at its own pace.

Ask Yourself: When was the last time you let a season slow you down? Not just physically, but emotionally?

Section 2: The Best Fall Foliage Routes and RV-Friendly Stops

Western Maryland: The Crown Jewel

Garrett County and Deep Creek Lake

Peak colors occur in mid-October. Highlights include Wisp Resort's scenic chairlift rides, Swallow Falls State Park, and Deep Creek Lake overlook.

Nearby RV Park: Deep Creek Lake State Park Campground offers full hookups, access to trails, and water views.

Catoctin Mountain Park

This area provides stunning vistas over valleys painted in orange and red, with popular hiking trails like Thurmont Vista and Chimney Rock. Nearby RV Park: Ole Mink Farm Recreation Resort, offering wooded sites and a peaceful atmosphere.

Scenic Drives Worth the Detour

Historic National Road (US 40)

Savage River State Forest Byway

Blue Ridge Summit Drive near Frederick

Travel Tip: Travel from east to west to follow peak foliage progression through late September to early November.

Section 3: Harvest Celebrations You Can't Miss

Pumpkin Patches and Family Farms

Butler's Orchard – Germantown

This location features hayrides, pick-your-own pumpkins, and corn mazes.

RV-friendly nearby: Little Bennett Campground

Baugher's Orchard – Westminster

Enjoy apple picking, fresh pies, and a petting zoo.

Nearby stay: Double G RV Park

Cider Mills and Apple Festivals

Weber's Cider Mill Farm – Parkville

They serve warm cider donuts, hand-pressed apple cider, and host an autumn market.

RV stay: Bar Harbor RV Park, about 30 minutes away on the waterfront

National Apple Harvest Festival – Biglerville (Just over the border)

Includes music, crafts, and orchard tours.

Well worth a short RV hop from Northern Maryland

Section 4: Cozy Fall Events and Small-Town Magic

Leaf Peeping and Community Spirit

Autumn Glory Festival – Oakland

This festival includes parades, craft shows, and antique car exhibits. A peak foliage location mixed with strong community pride.

Frederick's In The Streets Fall Celebration

Art, music, and food are celebrated in this historic downtown setting.

Nearby RV camping: Gambrill State Park

Evening Bonfires and Harvest Nights

Local vineyards such as Boordy Vineyards host evening tastings.

Many rural communities offer "Harvest Nights" filled with bonfires, live music, and local food.

Trigger Question: When was the last time you sat under a sky full of stars, the air smelling like woodsmoke, feeling full—not just from food, but from life?

Section 5: Tips for a Smooth, Soulful Autumn RV Adventure

Travel Timing and Foliage Forecasts

Use Maryland DNR's leaf tracker for peak times.

Avoid Columbus Day weekend traffic in western counties.

Packing Essentials

Bring flannel layers, waterproof boots, and a leaf blower for campsite cleanup. Warm bedding is necessary for chilly mountain nights.

Campground Tips

Book at least two months in advance—autumn is peak season for RVs. Choose sites with lake or ridge views to enhance your fall experience.

Section 6: My Most Unforgettable Fall Morning in Maryland

It was at Swallow Falls, early morning, fog hanging low, barely a soul around. I sipped my coffee—real coffee, not gas station brew—and just listened. The falls roared gently in the distance, leaves tumbled lazily from the sky, and the cold bit at my fingers.

I wasn't thinking about work, emails, or errands. Just the now. That rare, golden clarity that comes when nature strips everything down to what really matters.

You don't need therapy when nature's talking. You just need to listen.

Let Autumn Anchor You

Autumn in Maryland isn't just about beautiful views or apple pies. It's about returning—to the road, to the land, to yourself. With every tree that sheds its leaves, there's a silent reminder: it's okay to let go. It's okay to slow down. And it's more than okay to feel joy in the simple things—a sunrise over Deep Creek, cider shared with a stranger, or a warm blanket in a parked RV surrounded by flame-colored woods.

So tell me—are you just passing through this fall, or are you ready to belong to it?

WINTER ESCAPES AND COZY GETAWAYS IN MARYLAND

Where the Cold Finds You—and Warms You, Too

I never thought I'd fall in love with winter. I used to chase the sun, point my RV south as soon as the temperatures dipped below 50. But one December, something changed. I was driving north from Virginia, not really planning to stop in Maryland. Just a quick pass-through, I told myself.

Then I saw it: a dusting of snow over the Appalachian foothills, frozen lakes catching the last light of day, small towns wrapped in string lights and pine wreaths. I pulled over near a trailhead on a whim, layered up, and stepped out into the crunch of fresh snow underfoot. What I found wasn't just beauty—it was quiet, it was stillness. It was *peace*.

Have you ever stood in a place so silent, so hushed by winter's breath, that you could hear your own thoughts clearly—maybe for the first time in months?

This chapter is for the wanderer who thinks winter is something to escape. Let me show you that winter, especially in Maryland, is something to be embraced. From holiday markets to hidden cabins, from snow-covered hikes to cozy downtowns, this season has its own kind of warmth.

Section 1: Why Winter is Maryland's Best-Kept RV Secret

Maryland in winter might not be the first place that comes to mind when planning a cold-season RV trip—but maybe it should be.

Here's why:

Compact geography means you can move from mountains to the coast in hours
Off-season rates make RV parks more affordable and less crowded

Snow adds quiet magic to already scenic places

Holiday events and festivals bring charm without overwhelming crowds

Ask yourself: When was the last time you gave winter a chance to slow you down, not stress you out?

Section 2: Snow-Draped Adventures and Outdoor Wonders

Snowshoeing and Winter Hiking

Catoctin Mountain Park

Known for its quiet trails and stunning overlooks, it offers year-round access and fewer visitors in the winter months. Snowshoes or crampons are recommended after fresh snowfall.

Swallow Falls State Park

The frozen waterfalls here are otherworldly. Bundle up and take the trail loop—it's short, manageable, and worth every step.

Assateague Island

While most associate it with beaches and wild ponies, the off-season is peaceful and hauntingly beautiful. Brisk winter walks along the dunes offer solitude and ocean views.

Tips for Winter Trail Adventurers:

Dress in layers and stay dry

Check weather conditions before heading out

Keep a thermos of something hot in your pack—it makes all the difference

Section 3: RV Parks That Welcome Winter Travelers

Cherry Hill Park – College Park

Open year-round and close to DC for winter sightseeing. Full hookups, heated facilities, and amenities that stay active in the cold.

Deep Creek Lake State Park

Ideal for snow-based activities. Cross-country skiing, ice fishing, and cabin rentals available. A great base for a mountain winter experience.

Bar Harbor RV Park – Abingdon

A waterfront escape, even in winter. Quiet and serene, with beautiful views and easy access to small-town holiday celebrations.

Travel Tip:

Call ahead—some parks technically "stay open" but reduce services in winter
Bring heated hoses and insulation skirting if you plan extended stays
Propane management is crucial in cold months. Refill often

Section 4: Cozy Cabins, Fireside Retreats, and Comfort Food

Sometimes even RVers want a roof and four walls in the cold. Maryland's winter cabin options offer rustic charm without sacrificing comfort.

Savage River Lodge

Nestled in a forest of snow-covered trees, this eco-friendly lodge offers private cabins with wood-burning stoves. The silence here is meditative.

Caboose Farm Cabins

Located near Catoctin, these cabins offer easy access to trails and warm, welcoming interiors. Great for couples or solo reflection.

Wisp Resort Cabins

For those craving skiing, snowboarding, and cozy evenings, Wisp's accommodations near Deep Creek Lake are ideal.

Winter Warm-Up Essentials:

Stock your pantry with chili fixings, hot cocoa, and thick soups
Keep a basket of books or a journal handy—winter is a perfect time for reflection
A string of lights and a small pine wreath can make your RV or cabin feel like a holiday postcard

Section 5: Holiday Magic and Festive Small-Town Charm

Maryland's winter towns sparkle with old-fashioned charm. These aren't loud, over-the-top holiday hotspots. They're subtle, nostalgic, and wrapped in tradition.

Frederick's Holiday Nights

Horse-drawn carriages, candlelight shopping, and live window displays bring this historic town to life in December.

Annapolis by Candlelight

Tour historic homes dressed in holiday decor, followed by hot drinks at waterfront cafes.

Oakland Winter Fest

Includes a tree-lighting ceremony, local crafts, and snowy mountain views.

Boonsboro's Christmas Market

Local vendors, cozy bakeries, and a small-town vibe that feels straight from a movie set.

Ask Yourself: What if your next holiday memory wasn't about gifts or parties—but about slowing down, breathing in winter air, and feeling *present*?

Section 6: My Coldest, Warmest Night on the Road

It was the kind of cold that cuts through your clothes. My heater was on full blast, a mug of tea steamed beside me, and frost formed delicate crystals on the RV windows. But I wasn't uncomfortable. I was content. Outside, the world was still. Inside, I was warm.

I was parked near a ridge at Deep Creek, the stars out in full force, and everything felt right. No expectations, no plans—just the soft crackle of a space heater and the sound of snow falling on pine needles.

That night, I realized something simple but profound: winter doesn't have to be endured. It can be *savored*.

The Beauty of a Slower Season

Winter in Maryland doesn't beg for your attention. It waits for you to discover it. It rewards those who seek stillness, who travel with open eyes, who understand that some of the most meaningful journeys happen when the road is quiet and the nights are long.

If you're tired of the noise, the hustle, the race—then maybe this is your season.

Maybe it's time to park somewhere quiet. Light a fire. Sip something warm. And let winter remind you that rest is also part of the journey.

CHAPTER 12

CONCLUSION

YOUR UNFORGETTABLE MARYLAND RV JOURNEY

REFLECTING ON YOUR MARYLAND ADVENTURE

I. Opening Reflection: My Final Night Under the Maryland Stars

It was my last night in Maryland, and I remember it like a slow-motion reel, playing out under a sky soaked in amber and lavender hues. I was parked at a quiet, tucked-away campground near Assateague Island. The wind carried the scent of sea salt and pine. I sat on a collapsible chair just outside my RV, barefoot, tired, but inexplicably full—full of stories, full of awe, and yes, full of something deeper I hadn't expected to find on this trip: myself.

Have you ever had a moment so still, so stunning, that it broke something open inside of you?

I didn't go into this Maryland journey expecting transformation. I was just chasing a change of scenery. But somewhere between the misty mornings in the Appalachians, the Chesapeake Bay's soft lullabies, and the jolt of wonder from watching wild ponies gallop at the edge of the Atlantic—**I changed.**

This is not just a travel recap. This is a love letter. A deep, soulful exhale after a journey that cracked me open and rewrote my understanding of adventure.

II. The Road That Changed Me: A Recap of Your Maryland RV Odyssey

Let's pause. Breathe. Reflect.

Do you remember the way the air smelled in Deep Creek Lake just before sunrise? The way the light danced on the rippling water in St. Michaels? The eerie silence inside Fort McHenry, echoing with history and ghosts of resolve?

Here's a look back—your map of memories:

Western Maryland: The rugged serenity of the Appalachian foothills, where solitude met soul-searching. Did you feel it? That primal pulse in the earth that seems to whisper: "Slow down. Come home to yourself."

Central Maryland: Civil War battlefields, museums, roadside crab shacks, and bustling Baltimore nights. This region reminded me that **contrast is what makes life vibrant.** Tranquility and chaos. History and modernity. Silence and song.

Eastern Shore: The soft, sprawling flatlands of Chesapeake Country, where stories unfold in every shrimp boat, every sleepy town square. I found **community** here—strangers with open arms and eyes that smiled before lips moved.

Southern Maryland & Coastal Treasures: Point Lookout. Solomon's Island. Assateague's wild ponies. Each stop felt like discovering a new heartbeat of the state. Raw. Untamed. Magic that doesn't try to impress—because it doesn't need to.

III. The Seasons of Maryland: Why One Trip Is Never Enough

Maryland is not a one time fling. It's a **long-term love**, a place that shapeshifts with the seasons and always has something new to whisper to the curious soul.

Have you experienced Maryland in **autumn** yet? The foliage ignites like wildfire across the mountains, wrapping you in a kaleidoscope of color.

Or **spring**, when everything blooms with reckless abandon? Drive down Route 50 then, and you'll see fields that look like Monet spilled his soul across them.

Winter in Annapolis? Quiet, historic streets, fireplaces roaring in waterfront inns, and a subtle peace that descends like freshly fallen snow.

Each season, Maryland tells a different story—and **every single one is worth hearing**.

IV. Why This Journey Mattered (And Still Does)

This wasn't just about checking places off a map. If you've followed the route, you've probably realized by now: Maryland doesn't just offer destinations—it offers **emotional landscapes**.

Each curve of the road, each mile covered, pulled me deeper into **stillness**, into **introspection**, into **joy**.

I wrestled with loneliness in the Catoctin Mountains. I danced with strangers in a random beach party at Ocean City. I cried over an unexpected letter I received at a campground—because sometimes the road brings you back to the people you forgot you loved.

What did the road bring you?

Take a moment to write it down. Or whisper it to yourself. Or simply feel it. Because if you've really let Maryland in, you'll walk away not just with photos and souvenirs, but with a piece of it lodged permanently in your soul.

V. Tips for Returning (Because You Will Want To)

If you're anything like me, **you're already thinking about coming back**. And you should. Here's how to make your next journey even richer:

Return in a different season. Each one unlocks new routes, new challenges, and new kinds of beauty.

Stay longer in fewer places. Depth over breadth. Really get to know one region at a time.

Go off-grid. Skip the campgrounds with hookups sometimes. Find the quiet corners. The magic often hides there.

Document your emotions, not just your locations. Journaling, voice notes, sketching—capture how it felt, not just what you saw.

Invite someone you love. Or go solo again. But either way, make sure you're **present**.

VI. Your Next Step: Taking Maryland With You

Maryland isn't a dot on a map anymore. It's part of your story now. Whether you're back at home already or still parked somewhere along Route 301, you're carrying something with you—something intangible and powerful.

Let it fuel you. Let it remind you. Let it call you back.

Maybe your life needs more stillness. Or more movement. Or just more **you**, unfiltered and untethered.

What are you going to do with what you found here?

That's the real question. And only you can answer it.

VII. One Final Thought: This Isn't Goodbye

This isn't the end of your RV journey. It's a beginning wrapped in a farewell. Maryland has given you stories. Now you get to give them life.

Keep driving. Keep wondering. Keep returning.

I'll see you somewhere down the road—with mud on the tires, salt in the air, and your heart wide open.

PLANNING FUTURE RV TRIPS ACROSS MARYLAND

Explore more areas of Maryland on your next RV road trip.

Recommended routes for new RV travelers, with tips on itinerary planning and staying safe on the road.

I. The Journey Isn't Over—It's Just Getting Started

Let me be honest with you.

After my first RV loop through Maryland, I thought I'd seen most of what the state had to offer. I was wrong. Deeply, wonderfully wrong.

It wasn't until my **second**, **third**, and yes—**fourth trip** that I began to realize how **layered, surprising, and diverse** Maryland truly is. Just when you think you've uncovered all her secrets, she reveals a hidden cove, a forgotten trail, a roadside diner that serves life-changing peach pie and wisdom from a waitress named Carla who's been there since '76.

Have you ever felt like a place was speaking directly to your soul—inviting you back for more, not because you missed something, but because it missed you?

If you're feeling that pull, don't ignore it. **Maryland wants you back.**

II. Places Still Waiting to Be Discovered

Let's talk about the places you *might have missed*—the **quiet corners**, the **less-traveled routes**, and the **hidden gems** that don't always make the top-10 lists but can shift something in your spirit.

Patuxent River Scenic Byway

Tucked away in southern Maryland, this drive follows the Patuxent River through farmlands, marshes, and small historic towns like **Lower Marlboro** and **Waysons Corner**. It's peaceful, slow, and full of those **"I didn't expect this" moments.** Great for a weekend escape.

Mountain Maryland Scenic Byway (Alt Route)

If you only drove through Cumberland or Deep Creek Lake last time, this time take the **alternate roads that wind deeper into the Alleghenies**. Routes like 36 and 135 will lead you through coal towns frozen in time, hiking paths with waterfalls, and even off-grid camping spots no GPS will list.

Eastern Neck National Wildlife Refuge

It's not a classic RV destination—**and that's exactly why you should go.** Park outside, bike or hike in, and spend a day birdwatching or meditating by the water. It's pure stillness. A soul rinse.

III. Three Recommended Routes for Your Next Maryland RV Trip

Here are three **carefully crafted routes**, ideal for RVers looking to deepen their Maryland experience—especially first-timers or those wanting less stress and more magic.

1. The "Heartland & Bay" Loop (Beginner-Friendly)

Duration: 4–6 days

Route: Baltimore → Annapolis → St. Michaels → Cambridge → Blackwater NWR → Return

Highlights:

Easy-to-navigate roads and well-equipped RV parks

Waterfront towns with walkable charm

Culture, seafood, kayaking, and short scenic drives

Tips:

Reserve ahead in summer months

Plan lunch stops at public piers—they often have picnic areas and stunning views

Use local ferries when possible for a fun twist

2. The "Mountain Soul Search" Route (Nature & Reflection)

Duration: 6–8 days

Route: Hagerstown → Greenbrier SP → Catoctin Mountain → Frostburg → Deep Creek Lake → Swallow Falls → Return

Highlights:

Quiet hikes, crisp lakes, firepit nights

Ideal for digital detox or solo travelers

Historical small towns mixed with natural wonder

Tips:

Go in October for peak foliage

Prepare for limited cell service—bring analog maps

Don't rush. Stay 2 nights minimum per spot.

3. The "Wild & Water" Circuit (Adventure Lovers)

Duration: 5–7 days

Route: Ocean City → Assateague Island → Pocomoke Forest → Crisfield → Point Lookout → Return via Solomons

Highlights:

Beaches, forests, and marshlands

Wildlife watching, paddling, campfires on the sand

A little wilder, a little less predictable

Tips:

Book Assateague early—it's wildly popular

Pack bug spray and extra water

Respect nature rules—this trip is raw and real

IV. Smart Itinerary Planning: A Roadmap for Peace of Mind

You don't have to plan every second—but **a little strategy goes a long way.** Here's how I plan each of my RV trips now:

Start With a Theme. What do you want? Solitude? Seafood? Civil War history? Let your desire shape the map.

Choose 3–5 Anchor Stops. These are your "must-see" locations. Build the rest of your trip loosely around them.

Leave Room to Wander. Block off 1–2 free days to get "lost" on purpose. That's where the magic hides.

Check Road Restrictions. Some scenic byways have weight or size limits—**know your rig** and don't risk it.

Use RV-friendly Apps. I swear by **Campendium, Allstays, and RV Life Trip Wizard** for campsite reviews, dump stations, and real-world road conditions.

V. Staying Safe, Sane, and Inspired on the Road

You're not just a traveler—you're a **rolling home**. That takes a little extra preparation and mindfulness.

RV Safety Tips:

Inspect tires before every departure (blowouts are no joke).

Never push fuel limits—**rural Maryland can mean long gaps between gas stations**.

Level your rig properly—some of Maryland's most beautiful sites are on uneven terrain.

Mindset Tips:

Build in **non-driving days**—rest is not laziness.

Embrace slow mornings with coffee and quiet.

Journal every night, even just three sentences. Your future self will thank you.

VI. Your Next Maryland Chapter Awaits

You don't need to have it all figured out. You just need to have **the courage to go again.**

What part of Maryland is calling to you next?

Is it the haunted trails of Antietam?

The moonlit beaches of the Eastern Shore?

Or maybe the undiscovered stretch between La Plata and Leonardtown where the backroads hum lullabies?

Wherever it is—go.

Don't wait for a sign. This chapter is the sign.

Made in the USA
Columbia, SC
03 July 2025

Made in the USA
Columbia, SC
03 July 2025